THE ELVIS PRESLEY SCRAPBOOK

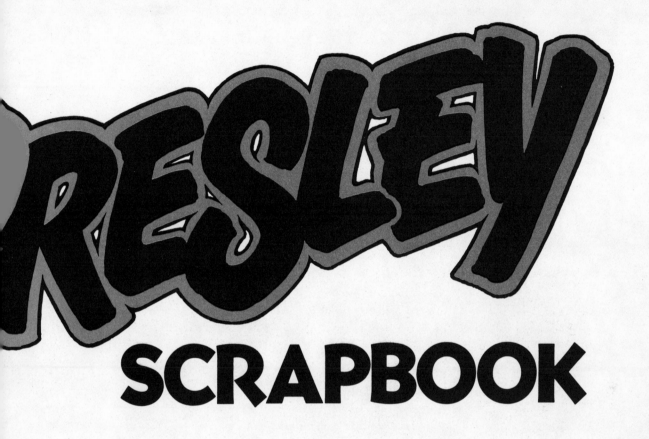

SCRAPBOOK

James Robert Parish

BALLANTINE BOOKS · NEW YORK

Picture Credits

NEA Service: pages 13, 23, 26

United Press Telephoto: pages 15, 29, 51 (bottom right), 53, 54, 56, 59, 64 (top left)

United Press Photo: pages 27 (left), 33, 51 (top)

UPI Telephoto: 60, 62 (top left), 64 (bottom left), 121, 123 (top right; bottom), 124, 153 (bottom)

Moss Photo Service: 63

UPI Photo: 65, 68, 72 (bottom), 154 (top right), 155

Bill Mark: 69

Las Vegas News Bureau: 83

Copyright © 1972 Metro-Goldwyn-Mayer, Inc.: 152

SBN: 345-24727-2-695

First Printing: October, 1975

Printed in the United States of America

Design by Karin Batten & Elliot Kreloff

BALLANTINE BOOKS
A Division of Random House, Inc.
201 East 50th Street, New York, N.Y. 10022
Simultaneously published by
Ballantine Books, Ltd., Toronto, Canada

*For Elvis, the Colonel
and everyone who has cared about EP
over the years*

Acknowledgment:
Research Associate: Gregory Mank
Editor: T. Allan Taylor
Research Assistants: John Robert Cocchi;
Florence Solomon; Ted Albert; Nancy Barr;
Bruco Enterprises; Mrs. Loraine Burdick;
James Butler; Kingsley Canham; Maria
Columbus; Carol Coyne; Morris Everett, Jr.;
Film Fan Monthly, Film Favorites, (Charles
Smith); Sharon R. Fox; Pierre Guinle;
Mrs. R. F. Hastings; Richard Hudson;
Ginger Johnson; Ken D. Jones; Sandra
Lelyveld; Ernest Leogrande; Mr. & Mrs.
Hilton Levy; David McGillivray; Albert B.
Manski; Mrs. Earl Meisinger; Jim Meyer;
Peter Miglierini; Movie Poster Service
(Bob Smith); Movie Star News (Paula Klaw);
Fred A. Parish; Michael R. Pitts;
Quality First Photos; Nick Rosa; Sean Saver;
Lucy Smith; Don E. Stanke; Charles Stumpf;
Jeanne Tessum; Robert Vaubel;
Ann Whitley; Don Wigal

On Memphis, Tennessee, on a hot Saturday afternoon in the late summer of 1953, a dusty Ford pickup parks at the curb in front of the Memphis Recording Service, where, for four dollars, anyone who walks in off the street can make himself a phonograph record. The driver of the truck—an eighteen-year-old aspiring country-music singer who makes $40 a week as a deliveryman for an electrical-contracting company—has often before passed the Memphis Recording Service. But now he's saved up four dollars and has it in mind to make a record of his singing and guitar playing as a surprise birthday present for his mother. Toting a battered guitar, he climbs out of the truck and goes nervously into the office, where, in a soft-spoken, rural Mississippi accent, he politely inquires about making a record. He'll have to wait his turn, he's told, for there are a number of others ahead of him and there's only a single recording studio. So, he plumps down on a wooden chair next to the desk of the receptionist-office manager, a cheery woman in her thirties named Marion Keisker. Lean, six feet tall, the youthful delivery-truck driver has a puffy, pouty, and yet not unhandsome babyish face that is dominated by sullen, heavy-lidded blue eyes. He has on a long-sleeved pink shirt with its collar turned up at the neck, tight-fitting black trousers, and a pair of black motorcycle boots. But perhaps the most notable aspect of his appearance is his exceedingly long hair and heavy sideburns—naturally dark-blond hair that is so lacquered with greasy pomades that it appears almost to be jet black. He wears his pompadoured hair in a so-called duckass cut and at once reminds Miss Keisker of the sort of motorcycle tough played by Marlon Brando in *The Wild One.* But he is soft-spoken and polite almost to the point of being unctuous—a sheep in wolf's clothing.

While the young man quietly awaits his turn to record, Miss Keisker has a conversation with him that she often has occasion to remember years later. "What kind of singer are you?" she asks him. "I sing all kinds," he says. "Well, who do you sound like?" she asks. "I don't sound like nobody," he replies. "Do you sing hillbilly?" she asks. "Yeah, I sing hillbilly," he says. "Well, what hillbilly do you sound like?" she asks. "I don't sound like nobody," he says.

When it is at last the young man's turn to record, Miss Keisker goes back to the studio to help him get set up and ultimately stays to listen to him sing. For his first number, he sings "My Happiness," a song that has lately been made popular by the Ink Spots, and for the other side of the ten-inch acetate record he does a teary ballad entitled "That's When Your Heartache Begins." On both songs, he accompanies himself on the guitar, creating an effect that— as he himself years later recalled—sounds like "somebody beating on a bucket lid." Within ten minutes, he has made his record, paid his four dollars and left. But Miss Keisker, who'd at once been extraordinarily impressed by his

Your Heartache Begins" on tape. And the following Monday morning, she gives the tape to her boss, Sam Phillips, who not only runs the Memphis Recording Service but is also the president of Sun Records, a small and struggling company that mainly puts out the records of black rhythm-and-blues singers. Phillips is as impressed with the young man's singing as Miss Keisker was. And so, although he doesn't yet know it, the young man's professional singing career has in a sense begun.

The summer of 1953. Eisenhower is President, Perry Como is the country's most popular singer, *I Love Lucy* is at the top of the TV ratings, and Norman Vincent Peale's *The Power of Positive Thinking* is a best-seller. A dull time in the history of America, to say the least, and a time, too, when most of the country's young are silent conformists in white-buck shoes and crewcuts. And so who could have dreamed that the young man who made his first record on that Saturday afternoon in Memphis would soon be one of the most influential national figures in changing the attitudes of America's young—to the point, in fact, where the *Sunday Times* of London would list him as one of "the shapers of the century"? Or who could have dreamed that within three years he'd be both the most famous and the highest-paid entertainer in the country? Or that he'd eventually star in thirty-one movies that would earn a worldwide total of more than $200 million? Or that, in 1975, he'd be getting $250,000 a week for performing in Las Vegas? Or that, finally, his records would sell in excess of 250 million copies—more records than the combined total sold of Bing Crosby, Frank Sinatra, and the Beatles? Who could have dreamed? Nobody. Least of all the young man himself, who was, of course, Elvis Aron Presley.

Elvis at age two

On 1935, Tupelo, Mississippi, pop. 6,000, was a rundown mill town in the middle of farm country in the northeastern corner of the state. It was the county seat of Lee County, and a couple of railroads ran through the town, but otherwise there was nothing in the least distinctive about Tupelo. And in the most depressed part of the town, East Tupelo, which was on the wrong side of the Mobile & Ohio Railroad tracks, a young couple named Gladys and Vernon Presley were then living on Old Saltillo Road in a two-room wood-frame house that was little more than a glorified shack. Gladys Presley, né Smith, was a $13-a-week sewing-machine operator for the Tupelo Garment Company, while Vernon Presley earned about an equal amount of money by working as a field hand on the farms around Tupelo. The Presleys were like figures out of one of Walker Evans' photographs for James Agee's *Let Us Now Praise Famous Men.*

PRESLEY BIRTHPLACE

Elvis Presley Youth Center and birthplace in Tupelo, Mississippi

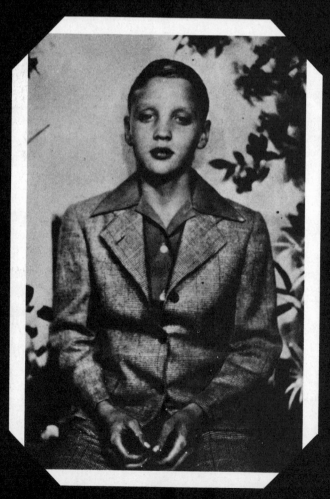

The young Elvis

With his parents

Elvis, cowboy-style

When they'd married, in 1933, Vernon had been seventeen and Gladys, an older woman, had been twenty-one, and shortly after noon on January 8, 1935, their first child was born. A son. He was one of identical twin boys, the second of whom was born dead. And they named him Elvis Aron Presley, after no one in particular although Vernon's middle name was Elvis. Perhaps because the stillbirth of her second son had made her frightened for the life of her first boy, Gladys Presley, who quit work in order to give her full attention to Elvis, brought him up as an extremely pampered and protected child. She rarely let him out of her sight to play with other children, for example, and she never went even down to the corner grocery store without Elvis in tow. Gladys Presley both doted on Elvis and spent endless hours teaching him to be well-behaved and polite—to always say "Yes, sir" and "Yes, ma'am" to his elders. And throughout the years of his childhood and youth Elvis was "a good boy" who never got into the slightest bit of trouble. It could even be said, in fact, that he was something of a mama's boy, for he doted on his mother as much as she doted on him.

While both Gladys and Vernon Presley could sing reasonably well, neither of them had any unusual talent for music. Nor was there a talent for music in either of their family backgrounds. (Their families, by the way, the Smiths and the Presleys, probably originally came to America from England, but no one knows for certain. "As far as I heard, us Presleys always come from around northeastern Mississippi, and so does the Smiths," Vernon Presley told an interviewer a few years ago.) From an early age, however, Elvis showed evidence of an exceptional singing talent. And by the time he was eight years old he was singing hymns with his mother and father at camp meetings, revivals, and at the Sunday-morning services of the First Assembly of God Church, which was one of the branches of a Pentecostal sect that the Presleys belonged to. When Elvis was ten years old, he entered a singing contest at the Lee County Fair, and won second prize—five dollars and a free admission to all the rides at the fair—for singing a maudlin song about a dog called "Old Shep."

When he was twelve years old, Elvis asked his parents for a bicycle, but they couldn't afford one. His mother, however, saved up some money and bought him a $12.95 guitar. At the time, he couldn't read music (and he still can't) and since there was no one around who could give him lessons on the guitar, he taught himself to play by listening to the radio and copying what he heard. A quiet, dreamy boy who had few friends, Elvis spent hour after hour listening to country music (i.e., hillbilly, as it used to be known) on the radio—to the records of Ernest Tubb, Roy Acuff, Jimmie Davis, and Jimmie Rodgers. And he also found himself peculiarly drawn to the music of such Negro blues singers as Booker White and B. B. King. Meanwhile, he continued to sing hymns at church. And he gradually developed a singing style that uniquely combined the sound of country music with that of Negro blues and old-time hymns. As he sang and played the guitar, he instinctively, too, began to move his body to the rhythm of the music in a way that imitated the twitching

Elvis and senior prom date, with his cousin, Gene Smith, and date

and gyrating movements made by the hell-fire Pentecostal ministers who preached at the First Assembly of God Church. Thus, he learned naturally to move in a way that within a few years would earn him a nickname that he particularly hated—Elvis the Pelvis.

As a field hand and worker at odd jobs around Tupelo, Vernon Presley had never made much more than a marginal living for himself and his family. But then, in the late summer of 1948, he found himself at once out of work and totally broke. And so, in desperation, he piled his wife, his thirteen-year-old son, and all of their meager belongings into a broken-down 1939 Plymouth and moved to Memphis, Tennessee, which is a hundred miles northeast of Tupelo. In Memphis, Vernon landed a job as a $38.50-a-week laborer in a paint factory and the Presleys soon settled into a tiny apartment in a federally-sponsored low-income housing project known as Lauderdale Courts. And it was there that they lived until Elvis struck it rich in 1956 on a scale that no one could possibly have imagined.

In the fall of 1948, Elvis Aron Presley entered Humes High School, in Memphis, which had a student body of 1,600, or more pupils than there had been people in all of East Tupelo. Overwhelmed by the size of the school, and being anyway a basically shy and reticent country boy, Elvis made only a handful of friends at Humes. And, majoring in shop, he wasn't much of a student, either. Nor did he make any kind of a splash during his high-school years. In fact, he passed invisibly through four years at Humes with few of his teachers or classmates later being able to recall ever even having set eyes on him. In his one attempt to enter into the activities of the school, he went out for the football team, but, weighing only 150 pounds at the time, he proved to be too light to make the varsity. And so, to his bitter disappointment, he was forced to quit the team.

Perhaps the only distinctive thing about Elvis during his high-school years was that he had long hair and heavy sideburns when just about all the rest of his classmates wore crewcuts. (Presley later explained that he wore his hair long in high school because he dreamed of being a motorcycler and also because, baby-faced, he wanted to make himself look older.) And he dressed differently from his classmates, too, in flaming-pink shirts, pink-and-black sports jackets, black pegged pants, and white shoes. Clearly, although shy, he had a deep yearning to be the center of attraction. But only once in his high-school years did he gain any special attention. In his senior year, he reluctantly agreed to play his guitar and sing in an all-school variety show that was put on before the entire student body of 1,600. More than thirty students performed in the show, but only Elvis —greeted after his song by a storm of cheers and applause—was called back on stage to do an encore. "They liked me," he said dazedly, with tears in his eyes as he came off stage after his encore, "they really liked me."

The Elvis D.A. and roll collar

Early publicity pose

On the club circuit, 1955

Of course, Elvis never for a moment considered going on to college, and for months before he'd been graduated from Humes High School, in June, 1953, he had a full-time ushering job in a downtown Memphis movie theater. And he soon moved on from ushering to work briefly as a factory hand for the Precision Tool Company. After which, in late July of 1953, he landed the truck-driving job (with the Crown Electric Company) that he was holding down when he made his four-dollar record at the Memphis Recording Service. At the age of eighteen, he dreamed of someday becoming a country-music singer, but he nonetheless sensibly covered his bets by enrolling in a night school, where he studied to become an electrician. At the time, Vernon Presley was earning some $2,000 a year as a laborer in the paint factory, and Elvis was determined that he wasn't going to wind up like his father. As an electrician, he reckoned, he'd at least have a profession for himself.

As noted, Sam Phillips was extremely impressed by the tape that he heard of Presley singing. Still, he was then working night and day to make a go of Sun Records, and he didn't get around to calling Elvis for months, even though Marion Keisker kept reminding him of "the kid with the long hair." And even after calling Presley to his office and listening to him sing in person, Phillips wasn't convinced that Elvis was yet ready to record professionally. Instead, he put Elvis in touch with Scotty Moore, a twenty-one-year-old guitar player, and Bill Black, a twenty-three-year-old bass player, and suggested that the three of them get together and see if they could work up a few songs to record. And for several months in the late winter and early spring of 1954, Presley, Moore, and Black met almost every night to play blues and country music. Finally, in June, they went back to Phillips and said that they were ready to record. Phillips listened to them play for a few minutes and agreed. Thus, in the tiny Sun Records studio at 706 Union Street on a night in the late June of 1954, Elvis Presley, backed by Moore on the guitar and Black on the bass, made his first professional recording. For the A side of the record, he sang "That's All Right, Mama," a song that had originally been written and recorded in the 1940s by Arthur "Big Boy" Crudup, a black blues singer whom Elvis had listened to on the radio for years. And then, for the B, or flip, side of the record, he did "Blue Moon of Kentucky," a bluegrass country-music song that had been made famous years earlier by Bill Monroe. The record of "That's All Right, Mama" and "Blue Moon of Kentucky" wasn't destined to be Number 1 on the charts or to sell a million copies, as so many of Elvis's later records did, but it was nonetheless a minor landmark in the annals of American popular music. Not only because it was Elvis Presley's first record, but also because it was the first record to combine the sound of white hillbilly music with the sound of Negro blues to form a unique new sound that would soon come to be known as "rockabilly."

Sam Phillips released "That's All Right, Mama" (perhaps a psychologically interesting title for the first song to be recorded by a young man with a galloping Oedipus complex) in August, 1954. To help promote the record, he took it around to Dewey Phillips (no relation), who was then one of the top disc jockeys at WHBQ in Memphis. Dewey Phillips agreed to play the record on a program called *Red, Hot and Blue,* and on the night that it was scheduled to be aired for the first time Elvis turned on the family radio at home to WHBQ for the benefit of his parents. But then, too nervous himself to listen, he went off to see a Tony Curtis movie. About halfway through the picture, however, his mother and father came breathlessly into the theater looking for him. Dewey Phillips had played "That's All Right, Mama" fourteen times in a row and the record was causing a sensation all over Memphis—scores of listeners had called the station to praise it and now Phillips wanted Elvis down at WHBQ to be interviewed on the air. Elvis bolted excitedly from the theater and ran all the way downtown to the WHBQ studios. At the station, he nervously told Phillips that he "didn't know nothin' about bein' interviewed." "Just don't say nothing dirty," said Phillips, and then, supposedly as preparation for the on-the-air interview, he proceeded to ask Elvis a number of questions about himself. Which he calmly and coolly answered. But what Elvis didn't know was that the microphone was already on while he was talking. "So, when's the interview start, Mr. Phillips?" asked Elvis. "It's already over, boy," said Phillips.

With Dewey Phillips, at WHBQ studios, Memphis, the first disc jockey to broadcast Elvis' recording of "That's All Right Mama"

The 1956 Elvis—ready for success

*E*lvis's record of "That's All Right, Mama" sold around 20,000 copies, got as high as third on the Memphis country-and-western sales charts, and even received national attention in *Billboard*, which described Presley as "a potent new chanter who can sock over a tune for either the country or r & b markets." Moreover, the record led to appearances by Elvis and his two back-up men on a number of country-music radio programs, including *Grand Ole Opry* and *Louisiana Hayride*, and also to invitations to appear in person at county fairs, schools, and small-town auditoriums. So, Presley quit his truck-driving job and chipped in with Moore and Black to buy a 1954 Chevrolet Bel Air. And off they went on the country-music tour to cash in on the success of their record.

It was while appearing on stage for the first time on that tour in obscure southern towns throughout Tennessee, Alabama, and Florida that Elvis first discovered that the twitching and

Elvis' first nationwide TV appearance, January 28, 1956, with the Dorsey Brothers on Stage Show

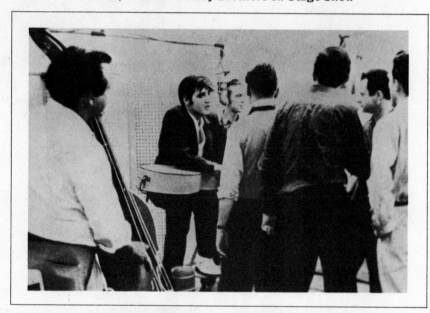

Gettin' it together at a 1956 RCA record session

gyrating he did while singing had a highly unusual effect on his audience. And especially on the teen-age girls in the audience. That is, his at first unconscious suggestive movements while doing a number like "Good Rockin' Tonight" turned them into screaming hysterics, of a type not seen in America since the squealing bobby-soxers who swooned over Frank Sinatra in the early 1940s. Before long, too, riots began to break out in the audience wherever Presley appeared.

As word of Presley's astonishing ability to turn on audiences spread through the country-music world in late 1954 and early 1955 he was soon booked into theaters and ball parks in cities like Jacksonville, Nashville, and his home town of Memphis. At first, he appeared on the lower half of a bill headed by country-music star Hank Snow, but he soon became the star of his own touring show. More and more riots broke out. In Jacksonville, for instance, a platoon of cops had to fight off a shrieking horde of teen-

Memphis, July 5, 1956: the Mr. Dynamite——Elvis Presley——demonstration at Russwood Park charity benefit

age girls who were battling to get up on stage in order to at least touch Elvis and maybe even to tear off a piece of his pink sports jacket.

Meanwhile, Presley made more records for Sam Phillips at Sun, with whom he'd now signed a long-term contract. In October, 1954, he made his second record, "Good Rockin' Tonight," which was slightly less successful than "That's All Right, Mama." In the first months of 1955, however, he recorded "Milkcow Blues Boogie," "I'm Left, You're Right, She's Gone," and "Mystery Train," and all three were smash country-music hits, if virtually unheard of outside the South.

From his records and public appearances, Presley suddenly found himself making more money than he'd ever dreamed of. And he spent it on a brand-new 1955 pink Cadillac and on setting himself and his parents up in a $40,000 ranch house in one of Memphis's more elegant neighborhoods. But the money he was then earning, some $2,000 a week, was only a hint of what he'd soon be making.

By the early fall of 1955, Presley had acquired a personal manager (a Memphis disc jockey named Bob Neal) and been voted "the most promising new country performer of the year" in a poll taken by *Billboard*; he'd also caught the attention far away in New York of RCA Victor Records. Indeed, in the person of Steven Sholes, who was the head of artist-and-

repertoire of the country-music division in Nashville, RCA moved in to buy out Presley's contract with Sun Records and take over the management of his recording activities. Before Sholes could sign Elvis with RCA, however, another party maneuvered himself shrewdly into the picture. A man who was to become the most important person in Presley's life aside from his mother. And he was, of course, the now legendary Colonel Tom Parker.

On 1955, Colonel Tom Parker—whose field-grade military rank was strictly an honorary one conferred on him in 1953 by Tennessee's Governor Frank G. Clements—was plump, waddling, and forty-five, a balding press agent, promoter, and manager of country-music singers who reminded more than one observer of a real-life counterpart of the sort of down-at-the-heels entrepreneurs played by W. C. Fields in movies like *Poppy* and *You Can't Cheat an Honest Man*. Colonel Parker, for example, was alleged to have once caught a flock of sparrows, spray-painted them yellow, and sold them as canaries. And he was also supposedly the creator of a carnival sideshow attraction known as the Dancing Chickens—under a bed of wet straw in a henhouse he'd placed an elec-

In Las Vegas, 1956

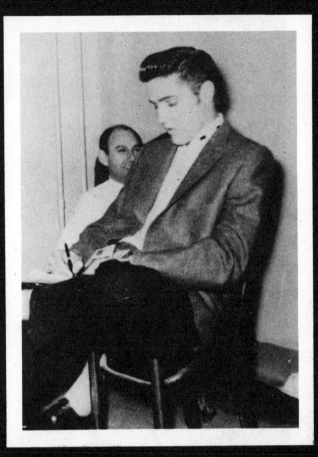

Backstage at Municipal Auditorium in San Antonio, waiting to go on

With "Uncle Miltie" on the Milton Berle Show, April 1956

Rehearsing for show with Steve Allen

Performing as usual

Elvis knockin' 'em dead in Fort Worth, Texas

"Weeelll Since Ma Baby Left Me"

tric hot plate, which, when switched on, caused the chickens to do something akin to the Charleston.

The Colonel was the son of carnival performers who died before he was ten years old. Taken in by an uncle who was also in the carnival business, he spent his childhood and youth working in various touring carnivals and small-time circuses all over the South. A short-order cook, a roustabout, he did everything—from selling hotdogs to reading palms to being the front man for a pony-and-monkey act. In the late 1930s, he'd married and given up the traveling life to settle down in Tampa, Florida, where he promoted country-music shows and so got to be chummy with such hillbilly stars as Minnie Pearl and Roy Acuff. Friendships which led to a job, back on the road, as an advance man for a touring show headed by Eddy Arnold, who in the early 1940s was one of the rising stars of the country-music world. And the Colonel proved to be such a successful advance man that he was soon promoted to Arnold's personal manager. In 1944, Parker negotiated a

recording contract for Arnold with RCA Victor, and a number of Arnold's records for RCA became major hits, including "Bouquet of Roses," which sold more than a million copies in 1947 and made Arnold the reigning king of country music.

In the early 1950s, after they'd been together for almost ten years, Parker and Eddy Arnold had a falling out, the upshot of which was that the Colonel found himself out of a job. After a couple of lean years, the Colonel landed on his feet again, hooking on as personal manager to Hank Snow, who by 1954 had replaced Eddy Arnold as the Number 1 singing star of country music. In the spring of 1955, when Elvis Presley joined the Hank Snow Jamboree for a ten-day tour of Texas, the Colonel had the opportunity to watch him perform show after show. And he quickly recognized the fact that Elvis had the potential to become an even bigger star than either Eddy Arnold or Hank Snow. He immediately wanted to become Elvis's personal manager, but Elvis already had a personal manager, of course, Bob Neal. Still, the Colonel recognized the fact, as apparently no one else had, that the way to Elvis Presley's heart was through Elvis Presley's mother. And so, whenever he was in Memphis, the Colonel took to making social calls on Mr. and Mrs. Presley in their new home, gallantly bringing flowers to Gladys Presley and impressing both parents with W. C. Fields-like flattery. Within a few weeks, he'd persuaded them that there was only one man in all of America who was qualified to guide their son's rising career. And that man, of course, was Colonel Tom Parker. He worked his wiles, too, directly on Elvis, and in November, 1955, at the urging of his mother, Elvis ditched Bob Neal and signed up with Colonel Parker. The terms of their agreement have always remained secret, but it is known that the Colonel cut himself in for at least 25 per cent of Elvis and that the figure may even be a good deal higher. Elvis also agreed to place himself entirely in the Colonel's hands—to leave all of the decisions about his career entirely up to Parker. And Elvis has done so right up to this day. For twenty years now,

Colonel Tom Parker has been 100 per cent in charge of Elvis Presley.

Of course, as a man who could foist off sparrows on the public as canaries and make chickens dance, the Colonel was eminently qualified to peddle Elvis Presley to the American people. Besides, to be perfectly serious, Colonel Parker had high-level connections in the country-music world and with companies like RCA Victor, connections that Memphis small-timers like Sam Phillips and Bob Neal simply didn't have. And Elvis was indeed in just about the best possible managerial hands. Now, with Colonel Tom Parker sturdily at the helm, Elvis's career, as 1956 began, was about to go through the roof.

Forget about Eisenhower's landslide defeat of Adlai Stevenson for the second time. Or the Suez crisis. Or even Marilyn Monroe's marriage to Arthur Miller. Nineteen fifty-six in America was the year of Elvis Presley. And no one else.

Before the year had begun, Colonel Parker had made a deal for Presley with RCA Victor Records whereby RCA bought out Elvis's contract with Sam Phillips and Sun Records for $35,000. And beginning in January, 1956, with "Heartbreak Hotel," one after another of Elvis's RCA releases not only became Number 1 on the charts in America but also sold more than a million copies. Among his incredible string of hits in 1956 were "Hound Dog" and "Don't Be Cruel," which were both at different times Number 1 in the country even though they were two sides of the same record—something that had never happened before and has never happened since. And in 1956 Presley also had Number 1 hits and million-copy sellers with "Tutti Frutti," "Money Honey," "Shake, Rattle and Roll," "Love Me Tender," and "Blue Suede Shoes."

In 1956, too, Presley symbolically stomped with his blue suede shoes all over Pat Boone's

"You Ain't Nothin' But a Hounddog"

With Richard Egan and Debra Paget in Love Me Tender

With Mildred Dunnock and Debra Paget in Love Me Tender

Publicity pose for Love Me Tender

On the set of Love Me Tender with Debra Paget

With William Campbell, Mildred Dunnock, and Richard Egan in Love Me Tender

24

Publicity poster for Love Me Tender (1956)

Lookin' very cool for 1956

"Presley for President" fans at Los Angeles Airport, 1956. Elvis had just arrived to make his first movie, Love Me Tender

Elvis in pensive mood

white bucks and all that they represented. Lowdown, raucous, and even explicitly sexual (e.g., "Good Rockin' Tonight" was not only about dancing), Presley's new rockability sound was running roughshod over the saccharine sound of songs like "Love Letters in the Sand." And maybe especially because their uptight parents were horrified by Elvis, America's teen-agers went wild for him and his music. For the first time, they had a music that was distinctively their own, with a beat and lyrics that reflected their yearnings for rebellion against the puritan and sterile adult world of Eisenhower, Levittowns, *Make Room for Daddy*, Eddie Fisher, Jo Stafford, Wonder bread, and the Edsel. In a sense, too, Elvis paved the way for Bob Dylan, for the Beatles, for long hair, for the sexual revolution, for the rise of the counterculture, and for all of the other revolutionary changes in life style that American youth brought about in the

1960s. But, of course, he did it inadvertently. All Elvis wanted to do was sing and make as much money as possible. For no one could be less politically conscious or socially aware than Elvis Presley.

Inevitably, as one Presley record after another reached the top of the charts, Elvis began to get offers to appear on television. And Colonel Parker eagerly snapped them up—for increasingly higher amounts of money. Presley made his first nationwide TV appearance in January, 1956, on Tommy and Jimmy Dorsey's Saturday night CBS *Stage Show* program, for a fee of $1,250. And he later returned to make five further appearances on *Stage Show*. In the spring of that year, he was twice a guest on the *Milton Berle Show*, for $5,000 each time. And that summer he was paid $7,500 for a single appearance on the *Steve Allen Show*.

Accustomed to singers like Perry Como and

Bing Crosby, American TV viewers had never seen anything like greasy-haired Elvis with his sideburns and duckass cut. Typically, he appeared on TV wearing tight-fitting, pink-striped black pants, a pink shirt with its collar turned up, and a drape-shaped pink sports jacket. And then, with his guitar slung low around his neck and his legs spread wide apart, he'd snap his right knee as he launched into a song—"Wellll, since mah bayy-beee left me/Ah've found a new place to dwell/It's down at the end of Lonely Street/It's Heartbreak Hotel." As he sang, he twitched both legs while undulating his pelvis in a manner that had previously been associated only with burlesque strippers. In other words, on nationwide TV he appeared to be imitating the movements of sexual intercourse (in *Newsweek*, John Lardner described him as looking like "a lovesick outboard motor"), and while teen-age girls across America were evidently all out having orgasms while watching Elvis, their parents were having conniptions. Indeed, a storm of anti-Elvis sentiment was soon sweeping America. Women's groups, PTAs, Catholic priests, rabbis, ministers (including Billy Graham), and political leaders angrily spoke out against Elvis and attempted both to have him kept off TV and to have his records banned from radio. "Appalling taste," said an outraged editorial in the New York *Times*, while a leading Catholic magazine, *America*, urged that the TV networks be forced to "stop showing such nauseating stuff." And the TV critics—most of whom, of course, knew absolutely nothing about country music—damned him as a totally untalented performer. "Mr. Presley has no discernible singing ability," wrote Jack Gould in the *New York Times*, and other critics were equally harsh on him.

In 1956, the highest-rated variety show on American television was Ed Sullivan's *Toast of the Town*, which was on for an hour on CBS every Sunday evening at eight o'clock. In those days, all of America watched Ed Sullivan on Sunday evening. When Presley had made his first appearances on TV, Sullivan, who was both politically conservative and a devout Catholic, had publicly said that under no circumstances would he ever have Elvis on his program. By the late summer of 1956, however, Presley was without doubt the biggest single attraction in American show business. And so Sullivan, who was above all interested in high ratings for his *Toast of the Town*, swallowed his pride and got on the phone to Colonel Tom Parker. Gleefully, the Colonel held Sullivan up for the highest pay that any TV guest had ever received—$50,000 for three appearances. Thus, on the night of Sunday, September 9, 1956, Elvis Presley appeared on Ed Sullivan's show. But Ed Sullivan didn't. He somehow couldn't make it that evening and was replaced at the last minute by the British actor Charles Laughton. Elvis's two songs in the show were broadcast as a live insert from the CBS studios in Hollywood, but as an indicator of exactly how uptight America was that year, Presley was seen—per the network censor's explicit instructions—only from the waist up. Still, even though America wasn't permitted to view his gyrating lower half, Presley's appearance on *Toast of the Town* gave the program the highest ratings in its history—an unbelievable 82.6 per cent of the TV audience, a percentage that in those days translated into

Christmas, 1956, in Memphis, with his parents and Las Vegas showgirl Dorothy Harmony

54 million viewers. And his two subsequent appearances on the show got it almost equally high ratings. Whether Billy Graham, Ed Sullivan, and others liked it or not, Presley was now ensconced at the top of the heap—the Number 1 entertainer in America.

Even before Ed Sullivan had signed up Presley, Hollywood had been after him. In fact, he made his first appearance on *Toast of the Town* from Hollywood because he was out there making his first movie, *Love Me Tender*, which was part of a $450,000 three-picture deal that Colonel Parker had negotiated for him with Twentieth Century-Fox. *Love Me Tender* was a Civil War story about the rivalry of two Southern brothers for the love of the same woman into which four songs and a death scene by Elvis were sandwiched. When the picture opened, in November, 1956, both it and Elvis were unmercifully panned by the critics. *Time* magazine, for example, described Elvis as looking like a cross between a sausage and a Walt Disney goldfish and as having about the same acting talent as a sausage. But the picture nonetheless packed them in all over the country and within weeks it had earned a profit of more than $2 million.

By the time that Elvis began his third movie, *Jailhouse Rock*, in the fall of 1957, the Colonel had upped his price to $250,000 per picture, *plus* 50 per cent of the profits. And by the middle of the 1960s Elvis was getting $750,000 per picture, again *plus* 50 per cent of the profits. In all, from 1956 to 1969, Elvis made thirty-one feature films, most of which were fairly inane musicals set in places like Hawaii, Acapulco, and Las Vegas, in which he starred as, say, a sensitive but misunderstood singing racing-car driver or a sensitive but misunderstood singing prize fighter who for some reason is constantly surrounded by a bevy of bikini-clad starlets. Still, the pictures, which did particularly well in rural areas, at drive-ins, and overseas, grossed a worldwide total of over $200 million and earned Elvis and the Colonel perhaps $25 million as their share of the profits.

After finishing *Love Me Tender*, Elvis topped off 1956 by making a nationwide singing tour during which he was paid as much as $25,000 for a one-night stand in a big-city auditorium or a ball park. And everywhere that he appeared in the fall of that year there were highly publicized riots of screaming and fainting teen-age girls. Followed by damning newspaper editorials and anti-Elvis magazine articles. America's love-hate relationship with Elvis Presley had become a kind of nationwide obsession.

Before going off on the tour with Elvis, Colonel Tom Parker had stocked up on thousands of eight-by-ten glossy photographs of Presley that he'd bought wholesale for five cents each. And now, wearing a change apron, the Colonel could be found in the lobby before and after each of Elvis's performances hustling the photographs at fifty cents each. Even though his cut of the receipts for the evening might be as high as $10,000, the Colonel simply couldn't resist the opportunity to make himself a fast extra buck.

While Elvis was earning millions in 1956 from his records, his TV appearances, his movie deals, and his personal appearances, the Colonel, in partnership with a merchandising expert named Hank Saperstein, had also shrewdly got Presley into the business of endorsing products with his name attached to them. And as the Elvis Presley industry boomed across America in late 1956, teen-agers were paying millions for Elvis Presley T shirts, sneakers, charm bracelets, stuffed hound dogs, perfume, lipsticks (in such shades as Hound Dog Orange and Heartbreak Hotel Orange), and two-dollar plaster-of-Paris busts of guess who. And Elvis's share of the take from the products, at an average of 6 per cent of the gross, amounted to around $600,000. Which, of course, was merely icing on the cake of an income for Elvis that in 1956 probably amounted to close to $10 million. Nineteen fifty-six. For Elvis Presley, it was a very good year.

And then came 1957. Once again, Elvis had an almost unbelievable string of Number 1 records that sold a million or more copies. Among them were "All Shook Up," "Teddy Bear," "Loving You," and "Jailhouse Rock." By 1957, too, RCA had issued two albums of his songs, and those albums became the first in history to sell more than a million copies. He also made a pair of highly successful movies—*Loving You* and *Jailhouse Rock*—in 1957, and he continued throughout the year to tour when not making pictures. And the Elvis Presley industry—a line of products to which stuffed Teddy bears, paper dolls, and coloring books had now been added—went on booming. And so Elvis probably earned as much in 1957 as he had in 1956.

By the middle of 1957, Elvis's biggest problem was to find ways to spend all the money he was earning. In July, 1957, he bought a $100,000 estate named Graceland on the outskirts of Memphis. The Graceland mansion was

That Presley smile

fronted by white colonial pillars, had twenty-
three rooms, and stood on a hilltop amid thir-
teen acres of private lawns. To keep out the
hordes of clamoring teen-age girls who now
turned up wherever he was, Elvis had a ten-foot-
high fence built around Graceland. And he also
put in an enormous swimming pool. Moreover,
he had the interior of the mansion redecorated
to include mirrored bedrooms with midnight-
blue walls, a motion-picture screening room,
and an outsize playroom in which there was a
pool table, a jukebox, a soda fountain (Elvis is a
lifelong teetotaler who never drinks anything

In Memphis with Hollywood starlet Yvonne Lime, April 1957

Quiet moment on the road

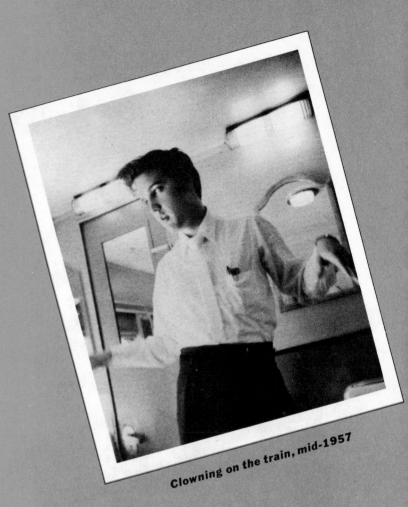

Clowning on the train, mid-1957

A cool dip

Rehearsal time

Won't you be——my Teddy bear

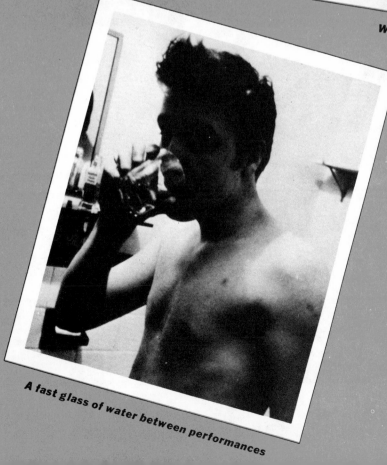

A fast glass of water between performances

On location with
Dolores Hart for
Loving You

Publicity pose with
Lizabeth Scott for
Loving You

Promotional item for Loving You

The star
of Loving You

With Dolores Hart,
Lizabeth Scott, and
Wendell Corey in
Loving You

In Loving You
(1957)

A pre-recording ses-
sion for Loving You
with composer-
conductor Walter
Scharf (left) and
dance director
Charles O'Curran

Lovin' 'em tender at a March 1957 performance in Fort Wayne, Indiana

stronger than ice-cream sodas and Pepsi-Cola), a piano, a couple of color TVs, and an expensive layout of stereo equipment.

And into Graceland he moved his mother and father, of course, plus his grandmother, an aunt, two uncles, and assorted other relatives. But perhaps the most talked-about group to take up residence at Graceland was a platoon of his old buddies from high school who soon came to be known as the Memphis Mafia. In their hairstyles and dress, the eight or so members of the Memphis Mafia closely modeled themselves after Elvis. And everywhere he went in 1957, from Graceland to Hollywood, Las Vegas, and the cities that he hit on tour, they lived and traveled with him. Each of them—"good ole boys" with

The audience

With Natalie Wood in Hollywood, 1957

Back to the grind

Elvis in action in **Jailhouse Rock**

ELVIS PRESLEY
AT HIS GREATEST!

His First Big Dramatic Singing Role!

HE SINGS 7 NEW SONGS

SINGING!
FIGHTING!
DANCING!
ROMANCING!

7 NEW SONGS!
Jailhouse Rock
Treat Me Nice
Young and Beautiful
I Wanna Be Free
Don't Leave Me Now
Baby, I Don't Care
One More Day

M-G-M PRESENTS

Jailhouse Rock

in CinemaScope · An Avon Production

SCREEN PLAY BY **Guy Trosper** · DIRECTED BY **Richard Thorpe** · PRODUCED BY **Pandro S. Berman**

CO-STARRING **Judy Tyler** · WITH **Mickey Shaughnessy** · **Dean Jones** · **Jennifer Holden**

Advertisement for Jailhouse Rock (1957)

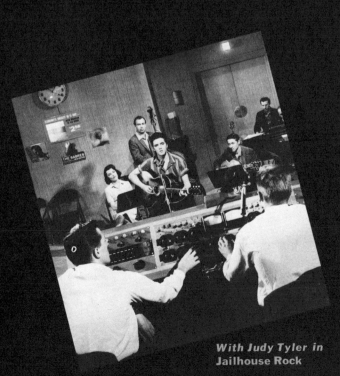

With Judy Tyler in Jailhouse Rock

With William Forrest and Jennifer Holden in Jailhouse Rock

Backstage at October 1957 San Francisco concert

Mrs. Presley and Elvis' one-time romantic interest Barbara Hearn backstage at Tupelo Fair

In 1957

names like Bobby "Red" West, Charlie Hodge, and Lamar Fike—was paid a salary of a couple of hundred dollars a week. For which they served as Elvis's personal squad of bodyguards as well as his chauffeurs, dressers, and errand runners. But he mainly kept them around in order to have resident playmates for the fun and games that he enjoyed when not working. They played touch football with him, for example, raced slot cars, flew model airplanes, and gunned motorcycles around the grounds at Graceland. On one occasion, Elvis and his live-in buddies bought out the entire stock of flashbulbs from every camera store in Memphis, threw them into the swimming pool, and then proceeded to make a day-and night-long game of shooting the flashbulbs in the pool with BB guns. "What Elvis liked was that there explodin' sound when you hit one of them flashbulbs with a BB—he'd laugh like a son-of-a-bitch," one of the participants in the flashbulb-shooting game later explained.

At Graceland, and at whatever Bel Air mansion he rented when in Los Angeles to make a movie, there was always a round-the-clock party going on. At the parties, Elvis, his buddies, and an endless succession of pretty girls sat around drinking Pepsi-Cola, watching TV, joshing, listening to records, dancing, and from time to time splitting off to bedrooms for rounds of sex. The girls—many of whom were recruited from

The pre-Graceland Elvis home, 1957

**With Carolyn Jones
and Walter Matthau
in King Creole
(1958)**

In King Creole

10216-20

With Dolores Hart in
King Creole

KING CREOLE

With Carolyn Jones in King Creole

Elvis and friends

Portrait of an American Idol, *painting by Italian primitive, Oscar De Mejo. The late actor James Dean is represented at upper left.*

Inspecting new wrought-iron gates at his Graceland home in Memphis

Elvis and guest Venetia Stevenson, Hollywood actress, in Memphis, 1957

With stripper Tempest Storm in Las Vegas, 1957

among the throngs of teen-agers who hung around night and day outside the gates of Graceland or at the doorstep of his rented Bel Air mansion—had one main object in mind: to go to bed with Elvis Presley. And there is every evidence that a considerable number of them suc-

ceeded, although most of them ended up being bedded down by one or another or all of the members of the Memphis Mafia. Or so claimed the Memphis Mafia.

By 1957, Presley had become so famous that it was no longer possible for him to go anywhere without being mobbed by his teen-age fans. So, when at Graceland, he took to renting a Memphis amusement park at night after it had closed to the public. With his buddies, plus whatever girls chanced to be on hand, Elvis would ride on the amusement park rides from midnight until dawn. His favorite was the Dodge 'Em cars, in which he and his friends would cheerfully scoot about for hours in the vast and otherwise deserted park. And he'd sometimes, too, rent movie theaters and roller-skating rinks for the night. In those days, Elvis Presley was essentially still an adolescent, with the emotional maturity of a thirteen-year-old boy.

As the money rolled in, Elvis spent tens of thousands of dollars on clothes, including a $10,000 gold suit. But his biggest expenditure was on cars, as he took to buying Cadillacs, Lincoln Continentals, and Rolls-Royces as casually as most men buy neckties. He also bought a small fleet of foreign sports cars, limousines, buses, pickup trucks, motorcycles, and go-Karts. On one occasion, he bought seven brand-new tractors on which he and the members of the Memphis Mafia staged races around Graceland. The result was that a number of the tractors were wrecked and lawns were torn up all over the estate.

Elvis obviously had far more cars than he possibly had any need for. They were parked all over Graceland, unused and virtually brand new, to be either sold or given away when Elvis had grown bored with having them around. More than once, the story has been told of a friend or even a stranger who admired one of Elvis's expensive cars and suddenly found himself the owner of it. "Hey, that's a beautiful Jaguar," someone might say to Elvis. "You really like it?" Elvis would ask. "Yeah!" "You got a dollar?" "Uh-huh." "Sold—it's yours!" And so went life for Presley in 1957—getting, spending, and giving away.

Army physician Capt. Leonard Glick giving Elvis his preinduction physical in Memphis, January 1957

On early 1958, shortly after he'd finished making his fourth movie, *King Creole,* something rather startling happened to Elvis Presley—he got drafted into the United States Army. For two years. And so, from an income of around $400,000 a month, he abruptly dropped down to a private's salary of $78 a month. Although, of course, the royalties from his records and the profits from his movies continued to pour in. Also, he'd recorded a backlog of songs to be released while he was away in the Army so that the record-buying public wouldn't forget who he was. Colonel Tom Parker, too, was laboring mightily on the home front to make certain that Elvis wouldn't be forgotten. "I consider it my patriotic duty," said the Colonel, "to keep Elvis in the ninety-per-cent tax bracket while he's in the Army." Still, there were many of his detractors who believed that when Elvis entered the Army, on March 24, 1958, his career—thank God—was over. Presley, they claimed, was a faddish figure who would be all but forgotten in

United States Army swearing-in, Memphis, March 24, 1958

two years. This turned out to be wishful thinking on their part, however, for Elvis's popularity scarcely diminished at all during his military service.

On the advice of Colonel Parker, Elvis chose not to become an entertainer in the Army's Special Services as the Pentagon had hoped he'd be—but instead to be simply a regular soldier. And so, along with a bunch of other recruits, he was sent first to Fort Chaffee, Arkansas, where the most publicized haircut of 1958 took place —Elvis's long hair and sideburns were shorn off with electric clippers. And, sporting a crewcut, off he went to Fort Hood, Texas, for eight weeks of basic training.

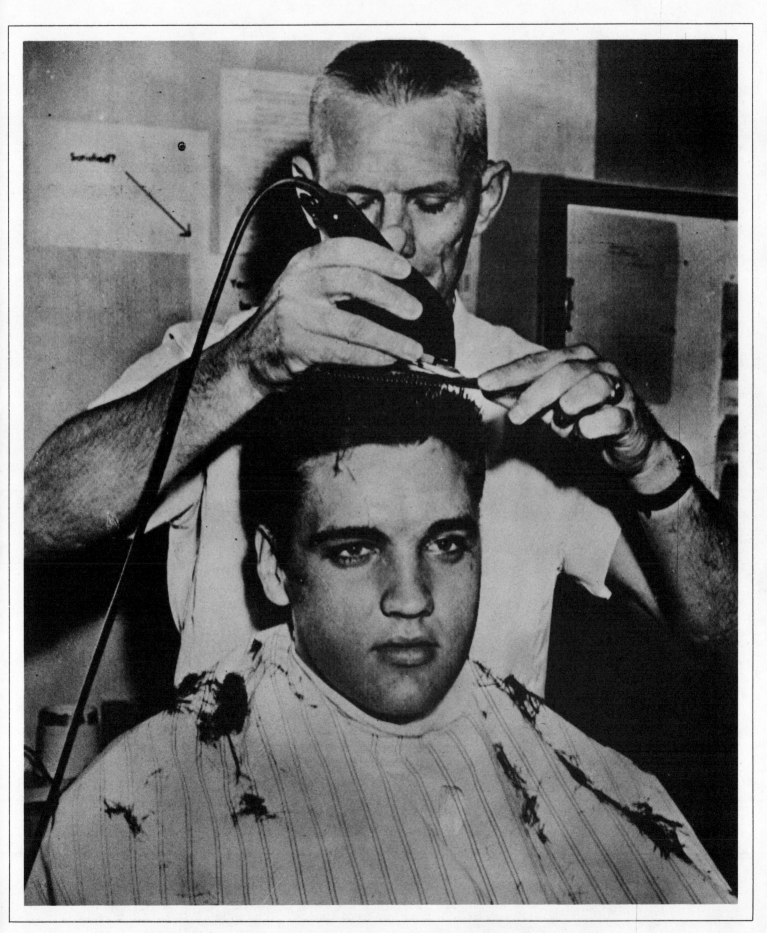

The famous Presley D.A. gives way to regulation Army crewcut, administered by James Peterson at Fort Chaffee, Arkansas, March 25, 1958

Sfc. Calvin Rhoades giving Asiatic flu shot to Private Elvis, March 26, 1958

After basic and a seven-day leave back home at Graceland, Elvis returned to Fort Hood to undergo eight weeks of armored training, and it was then that something genuinely tragic happened to Elvis for perhaps the first time in his life: his mother died.

For a long time, Gladys Presley, who was forty-six when she died, on August 14, 1958, had been seriously overweight. And, especially in front of her famous son, she'd been desperately ashamed of it. So she'd got herself some diet pills, which were actually amphetamines, and mixed them with the enormous amount of alcohol that she'd been downing in her depression over being fat. The official cause of her death was given as a heart attack, but it's highly

Elvis battling his duffel bag at Fort Chaffee, March 31, 1958

A slim and trim Elvis boards Navy transport in Brooklyn for European duty, September 22, 1958

probable that it was actually from a fatal mixture of drugs and alcohol. "It was real sad," a close family friend later recalled for an interviewer. "Gladys only wanted to make Elvis proud of her. She just wanted him to be proud. But she kept on taking those pills, and drinking..."

Elvis reached his mother's bedside moments after she died in a Memphis hospital, and he stayed alone with her dead body for only a minute or two. Then he came stoically out,

walked down a hall to an empty waiting room, slumped down in a chair, and burst into tears. A couple of days later, after his mother had been buried, Elvis and his father stood together for a time on the front steps at Graceland. "Look, Daddy," sobbed Elvis, pointing to chickens that his mother had kept on the front lawn of the estate, "Mama won't never feed them chickens no more." And on her gravestone Elvis later had these words inscribed: "She was the sunshine of our house."

Arriving in Frankfurt, West Germany, for Army posting

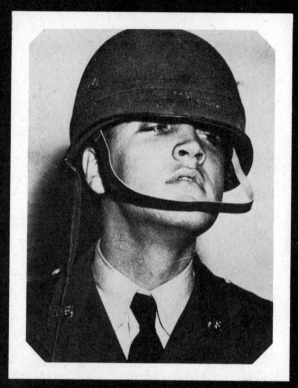

Trying out steel helmet, part of new gear issued at Army base in Friedberg, West Germany, October 3, 1958

Pvt. Elvis Presley

G.I. Elvis with parents

Best Wishes
Elvis Presley

Elvis in uniform

March 5, 1960—Elvis
musters out

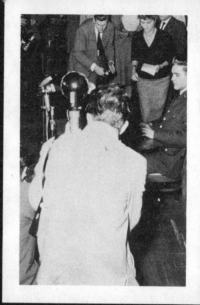

News conference on arrival back
in the U.S., March, 1960

With Margrit Buergin, of Frankfurt, his

With his father at the Ritters Park Hotel in

Nancy Sinatra presenting Elvis with gift from her famous father at Fort Dix,
New Jersey, March 3, 1960

In late September of 1958, as the press swarmed around the Military Ocean Terminal in Brooklyn and an Army band played "All Shook Up," Elvis sailed off to Germany on a troop ship. And he spent the rest of his fairly uneventful military career as a scout Jeep driver assigned to an armored unit stationed in Friedberg, Germany, not far from Frankfurt. Said Elvis's top sergeant, "He scrubs, washes, greases, paints, marches, runs, carries his laundry, and worries through inspections just like everyone else." In short, Elvis got no special or favored attention while in the Army, although he lived off base in Friedberg with his widowed father, who'd come to Germany to keep him company.

In early March, 1960, Elvis was flown back from Germany with a planeload of other troops to Fort Dix, New Jersey, where—with a good deal of hoopla that had been arranged by Colonel Parker—he was honorably discharged from the Army with the rank of sergeant. He'd been a good soldier.

With producer Hal B. Wallis, discussing Elvis' first post-Army Hollywood feature

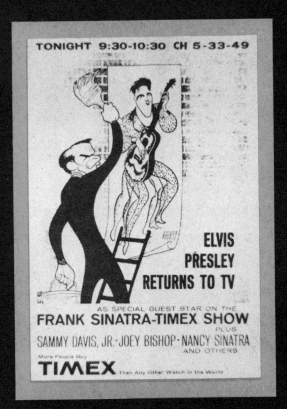

TV Guide *announcement for May 12, 1960,*
Timex show

*B*ack in civilian life, Presley pretty much
picked up his career where he'd dropped
it in 1958. He immediately began making records again, for instance, and he amazingly soon
had yet another string of Number 1 hits and
million-copy sellers, including "It's Now or
Never" and "Are You Lonesome Tonight?" What
was significant about these new hits, however,
was that they weren't rock 'n' roll numbers but
ballads, of the sort that Pat Boone or Perry
Como could just as easily have recorded. The
reason: Colonel Parker had made a command
decision that rock 'n' roll was dead and that
Elvis could only survive by going along with
what the mass public wanted. Which, of course,
was exactly the opposite of the way that he'd got
to the top in the first place. Still, as always, Presley did what the Colonel told him to do.

Shortly after getting out of the Army, Elvis
picked up $125,000 for doing six minutes on a
Frank Sinatra TV special, and he then headed
off to Hollywood to make his first post-Army

Priscilla Beaulieu plays an Elvis record at home in Wiesbaden, West Germany. Miss Beaulieu, daughter of an Air Force captain, was Elvis' steady date in early 1960

movie, entitled, appropriately enough, *G.I. Blues.* The new picture, which was simultaneously released in more than five hundred theaters in October, 1960, turned out to be a service farce with a score of Tin Pan Alley-type songs that sounded as though they might have come from a 1940s' Doris Day musical. "When they took the boy out of the country, they apparently took the country out of the boy," said Jim Powers in the *Hollywood Reporter.* "It is a subdued and changed Elvis Presley who has returned from military service in Germany to star in Hal Wallis's *G.I. Blues.*" And, added Powers, "the picture will have to depend on the loyalty of

The puppet sequence of G.I. Blues

On the set of G.I. Blues with Shirley MacLaine

With Juliet Prowse in G.I. Blues

Babysitter Elvis in G.I. Blues

With James Douglas, Mickey Knox, and Arch Johnson in G.I. Blues

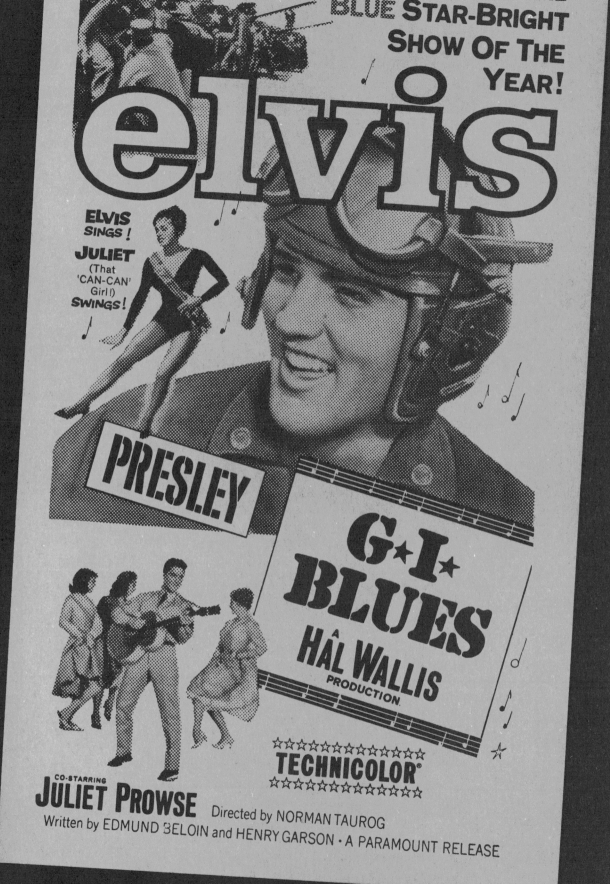

Advertisement for G.I. Blues (1960)

Candid shot taken in 1960

Teasing the press at news confere
in Beverly Wilshire Hotel, 196C

Being inducted into the Los Angeles Indian Tribal Council by Chief Wah-Nee-Ota,
December 1960, in recognition for his "constructive portrayal of a man of
Indian blood" in 20th Century-Fox's Flaming Star

Back home and swamped, as usual, by his fans

Presley fans to bail it out at the box office." And bail it out they did, for *G.I. Blues* grossed $4.3 million in the United States and Canada alone and was one of 1960's biggest box-office hits. But even his most dedicated fans agreed that a new Elvis had emerged in *G.I. Blues*—the days of the long hair, of the gyrating pelvis, and of "Good Rockin' Tonight" were apparently gone for good. Which was exactly as Colonel Parker wanted things—the image of Presley as the easygoing regular guy who cheerfully did his hitch in the Army was now also to be his image

On the set of Flaming Star with director Don Siegel

Advertisement for Flaming Star (1960)

With Rudolph Acosta in Flaming Star

With Dolores Del Rio in Flaming Star

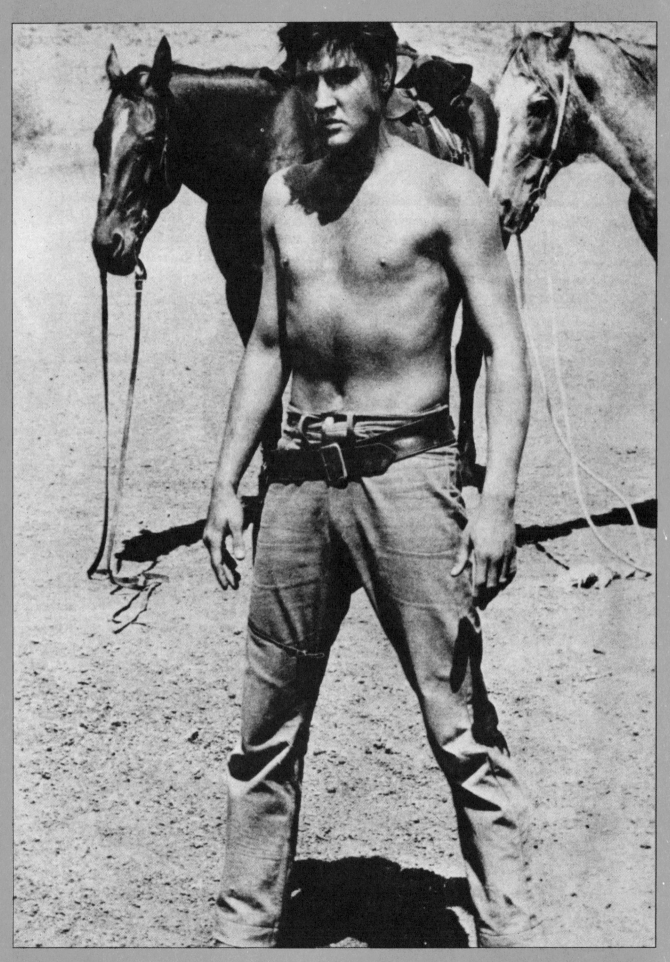

As Pacer in Flaming Star

Elvis ! Army recognizes :

Private ~~Sharon Fox~~ Serial
as a loyal member

No. ~~1227~~

Linda Pearson: Sgt.
4302 Gertrude Drive
Fremont, California

May 62 -
May 6

"Our King" E.P.F.C.
THIS IS TO CERTIFY THAT

Sharon Fox

IS A LOYAL ELVIS FAN.

JOYCE BUCKNELL
PRESIDENT

This Certifies That

SHARON FOX

Is A Member of The

NOW AND FOREVER
ELVIS PRESLEY FAN CLUB

CAROLE BENSON, President

ELVIS PRESLEY, Honorary President

Expires 5/8/62

Growth of the Elvis Presley fan clubs

Official Elvis Presley Fan Club
8403 BAY ROAD,   RIVIERA BEACH, MARYLAND

NAME
SHARON FOX
ACTIVE

DATE
NOVEMBER 10, 195

"ELVIS IS OUR CAUSE"

Elvis Presley
HONORARY PRESIDENT

Linda
ACTIVE PRE

EVER

OFFICIAL * NATIONAL
E. P. CONTINENTALS

LOYAL

This certifies that

Sharon Fox

is a member in Good Standing
MOTTO "THE CLUB ELVIS NAMED"

Date *Sept 13 1961*

CO-PRESIDENTS — JEAN AND PAM DREW
Chicago, Ill.

TO HON. PRES. "ELVIS"

E.P. CONTINENTALS
JEAN AND PAM DREW
2915 S. Eastout Ave.
CHICAGO 22, ILL.

in the movies and on records. In short, Colonel
Parker was calculatedly turning Elvis into a
kind of latter-day Bing Crosby.

For a long time, the new Elvis seemed to be
just as successful as the old Elvis with his loyal
public, who were themselves now a bit more

With Tuesday Weld in Wild in the Country

With Millie Perkins in Wild in the Country

With Hope Lange in Wild in the Country

On the set of Wild in the Country *with Colonel Parker (center) and director Philip Dunne*

With William Mims, John Ireland, and Hope Lange in Wild in the Country

ELVIS PRESLEY

SINGS OF LOVE TO
**HOPE TUESDAY MILLIE
LANGE · WELD · PERKINS**

JERRY
WALD'S
production of

**WILD
IN THE
COUNTRY**

20th
CENTURY-FOX

CinemaScopE
COLOR by DE LUXE

co-starring
RAFER JOHNSON · JOHN IRELAND
Directed by   Screenplay by
PHILIP DUNNE · CLIFFORD ODETS

"I'm not a postage stamp you just cancel out!"

"You're wild, just like me ...that's why we belong together!"

"I'm yours... for the rest of my born days!"

STARTS FRIDAY! **PARAMOUNT**
Broadway & 43rd Street

Dispensing with his guitar for a moment, Elvis swings a mean right——and connects

With Joan Blackman (in water) in Blue Hawaii

With Joan Blackman, Roland Winters, and Angela Lansbury in Blue Hawaii

On the set of Blue Hawaii (1961) with Barbara Walters (at table, left) and Joan Blackman (right of Presley)

Blue Hawaii

With Joan Blackman in Blue Hawaii

With Colonel Parker and Memphis Mayor Henry Loeb, 1961

On location in Seattle for It Happened at the World's Fair, 1962

With friend Johnny Cash in 1961

Belated twenty-seventh-birthday salute for Elvis in Las Vegas from his friend, hotelman Milton Prell

mellow than they'd been in 1956. Throughout the 1960s, Elvis continued to make his movies, lightweight musicals with titles like *Girl Happy, Tickle Me, Paradise—Hawaiian Style;* and *Harum Scarum* in which he was co-starred with the likes of Shelley Fabares, Ann-Margret, Mary Ann Mobley, and Nancy Kovack. And for quite a while the pictures continued to make money. In 1966, for example, Presley earned $5 million, most of which came from his movies.

Still, Elvis's career went into a decline in the 1960s, and from the spring of 1962 until the

The informal Elvis

winter of 1969 he didn't have a single Number 1 record. The problem was that a new generation of teen-agers had come along who were into Bob Dylan, the Beatles, the Rolling Stones, and the hard-rock sound of groups like the Jefferson Airplane. And who looked upon Elvis as a back number, even though many of the most popular singers and groups of the 1960s, including the Beatles, admitted to having been heavily influ- enced by Elvis. From 1962 to 1969, moreover, Elvis made no public appearances. He divided all of his time between Graceland and various Los Angeles houses that he rented. And he once again took up the life style that he'd led before going into the Army. The nonstop parties—com- plete with the Memphis Mafia, the girls, and the Pepsi-Cola—were resumed. Once more, too, it was fun-and-games time, complete with a live-

Christmas greetings, G.I. and civilian style

Elvis and the Colonel in Hollywood, 1962

in pet chimpanzee, water-pistol fights, and flame-thrower fights (with butane lighters Elvis and his buddies cut the ends off of).

But if he went in for a good deal of childish horseplay, Elvis still didn't drink, or smoke anything stronger than an occasional small Dutch cigar, and his only vice, aside from a penchant for womanizing, was a serious tendency to over-eat. And he ate almost nothing but junk— cheeseburgers, French fries, peanut-butter-and-banana sandwiches, and burnt bacon were

his favorite foods. From such a diet, Elvis began to put on a good deal of weight in the mid 1960s, which then led him to go on a series of crash programs to lose it. But he nonetheless gradually got fatter, to the point where he could no longer stand to look at himself in his movies. He grew sullen, reclusive, and uncharacter-istically mean-tempered. He kicked in the fronts of several TV sets, smashed a pool table, broke up an expensive guitar, and on one occa-sion, when he'd arrived home late to find the

★ ELVISGRAM ★

ELVIS PERFORMS FOR CHARITY
FEBRUARY 25, 1961 — *MEMPHIS*
  ELVIS DID SHOW RAISING SUM OF
    $52,000 — ALL WENT TO CHARITY
MARCH 25, 1961 — HAWAII
  ELVIS' SHOW RAISES $67,000 FOR BENEFIT
    OF ARIZONA WAR MEMORIAL

AWARDSVILLE FOR THE KING
APRIL 1961 NATIONAL RECORD MANUFACTURERS
  ASSOCIATION GAVE THE FOLLOWING AWARDS
(1) BEST MALE ARTIST OF 1960 — ELVIS PRESLEY
(2) BEST SONG 1960 "NOW OR NEVER" BY ELVIS
(3) BEST SELLING LP 1960 GI BLUES BY ELVIS

1960-1961   ELVIS WINS
17 AWARDS IN TV AND RADIO POLLS
ELVIS SWEEPS AMERICAN BANDSTAND 5TH YR.
WINS 12 AWARDS — MAGAZINES AND PAPER POLLS
FOR 5TH YEAR
ELVIS WINS ANNUAL EUROPEAN POPULARITY POLL
  LOS ANGELES MIRROR ANNUAL MUSIC POLL
  TV STAR PARADE POLL

DID YOU KNOW ?
ELVIS HAS 39 GOLD RECORDS
  FOR MILLION SELLERS
ELVIS' TOTAL RECORD SALES
  TO DATE — 77 MILLION !!

COMPILED BY: HELEN HUBER, CHICAGO, ILL.
PRINTED BY: MILDRED EATON, CHANNELVIEW, TEX.

Keeping the public alerted to Elvis' accomplishments

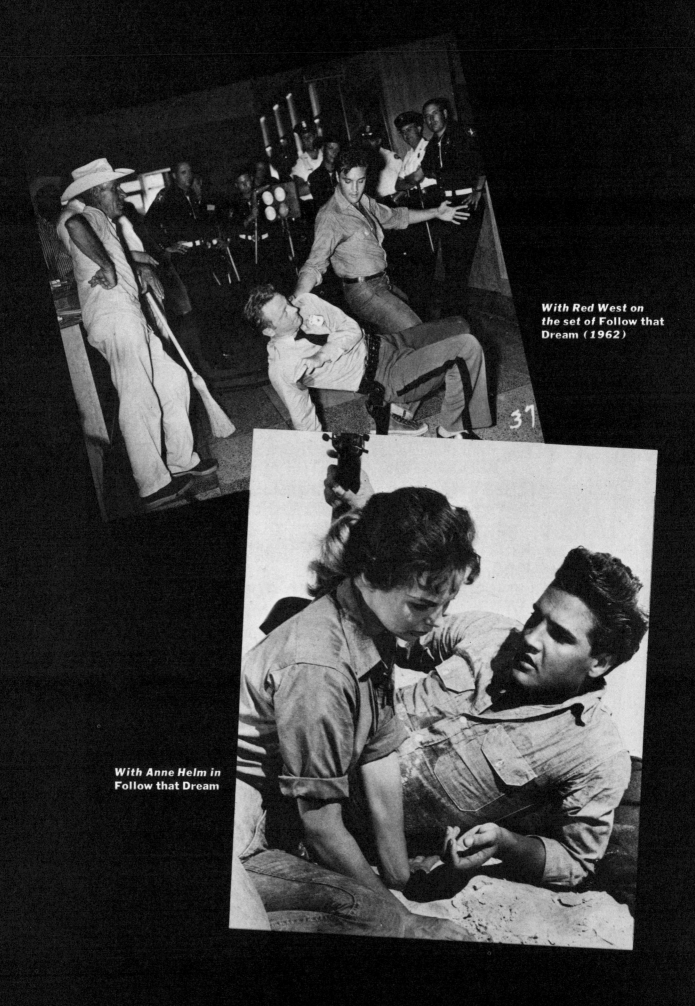

With Red West on
the set of Follow that
Dream (1962)

With Anne Helm in
Follow that Dream

Follow that

With Anne Helm, Arthur O'Connell, and the "brood" in publicity shot for Follow that Dream

Dream

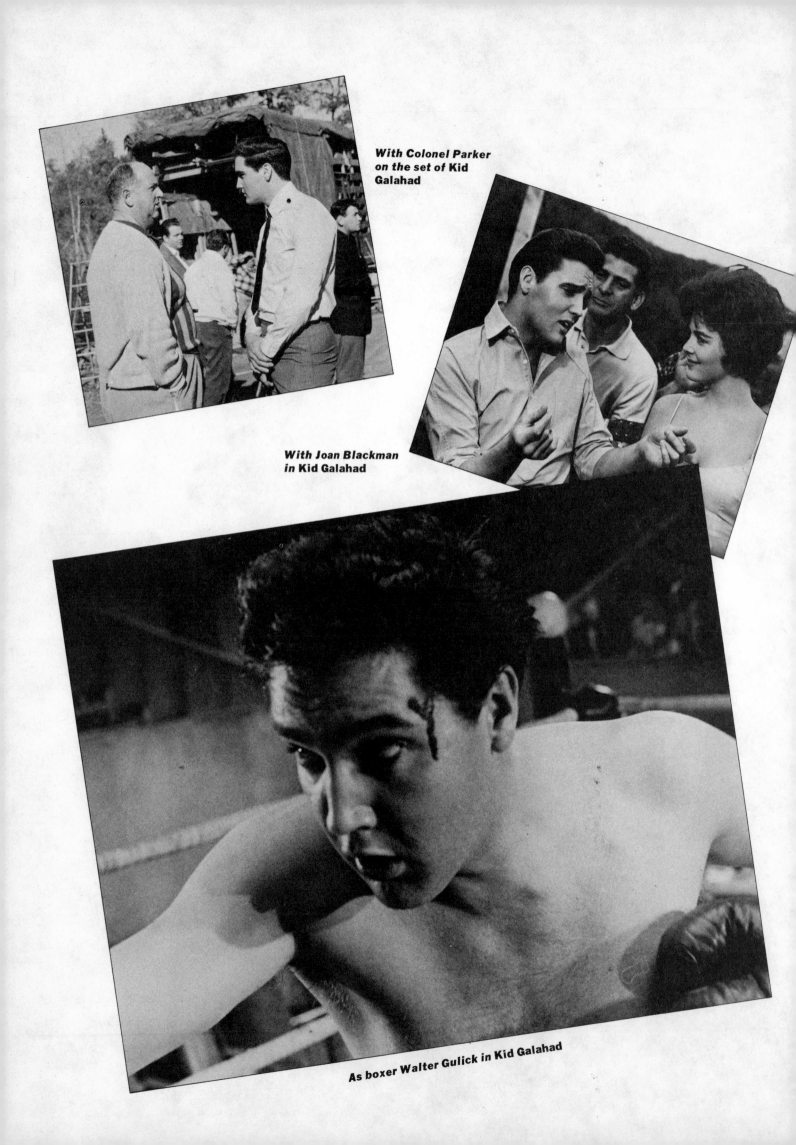

With Colonel Parker on the set of Kid Galahad

With Joan Blackman in Kid Galahad

As boxer Walter Gulick in Kid Galahad

With Joan Blackman and Lola Albright in a publicity pose for Kid Galahad (1962)

With Jeremy Slade in Girls! Girls! Girls!

On the set of Girls! Girls! Girls!

With Laurel Goodwin in Girls! Girls! Girls! (1962)

With Ginny and Elizabeth Tiu, and Laurel Goodwin in Girls! Girls! Girls!

SELL THE KIDS VIA
COLORING CONTEST

Coloring contests always go over big with the younger set. Aim for that market by planting this specially prepared art in the newspaper and/or getting a cooperating store to use it in herald form as package stuffers. Offer guest tickets, records and any other prizes you can promote to the first so-many most attractively colored entries.

(Copy for contest)

HEY, KIDS! COLOR THIS SCENE FROM "GIRLS! GIRLS! GIRLS!" . . . YOU MAY WIN TICKETS TO SEE THE NEW ELVIS PRESLEY MUSICAL . . . PLUS OTHER PRIZES!

See how good an artist you are! Send your completed picture to Contest Editor at this paper no later than . . . .

(date)

Promotional material for Girls! Girls! Girls!

**With Yvonne Craig in
It Happened at the
World's Fair**

It Happened at the World's Fair

On location in Seattle for It Happened at the World's Fair

With Joan O'Brien in It Happened at the World's Fair (1963)

With Vicky Tiu in It Happened at the World's Fair

In Fun in Acapulco

**With Ursula Andress
and Paul Lukas in
Fun in Acapulco**

**With Ursula Andress
and Larry Domasin
in Fun in Acapulco**

96

In Fun in Acapulco (1963)

FUN IN ACAPULCO

With Glenda Farrell and
Arthur O'Connell (right)
in Kissin' Cousins

Kissin' Cousins

As Josh Morgan
and Jodie Tatum in
Kissin' Cousins (1964)

With Yvonne Craig and Pamela Austin in publicity pose for Kissin' Cousins

With Ann-Margret in Viva Las Vegas

With Ann-Margret in Viva Las Vegas

With Nicky Blair, Roy Engel, William Demarest, and Ann-Margret in Viva Las Vegas

Advertisement for
Viva Las Vegas
(1964)

With Barbara Stanwyck in Roustabout

With Sue Ane Langdon in Roustabout

With Barbara Stanwyck, Joan Freeman, and Leif Erickson in Roustabout

Advertisement for Roustabout (1964)

With Jimmy Hawkins, Gary Crosby, and Joby Baker in Girl Happy

Singing and dancing the Crab with Shelley Fabares, while Jimmy Hawkins plays guitar in Girl Happy

With Lynn Edginton, Chris Noel, Shelley Fabares, and John Fiedler in Girl Happy

Advertisement for
Girl Happy (1965)

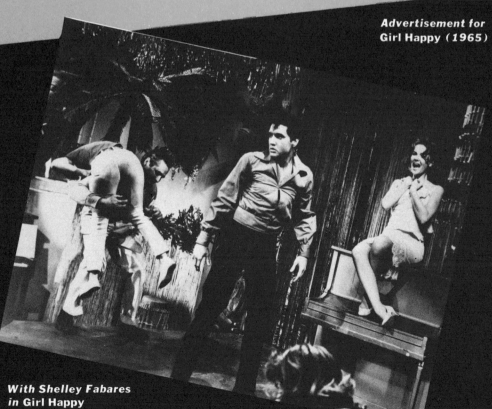

*With Shelley Fabares
in Girl Happy*

**With Jocelyn Lane
and Jack Mullaney in
Tickle Me**

**As Lonnie Beale in
Tickle Me**

In Tickle Me (1965)

TICKLE ME

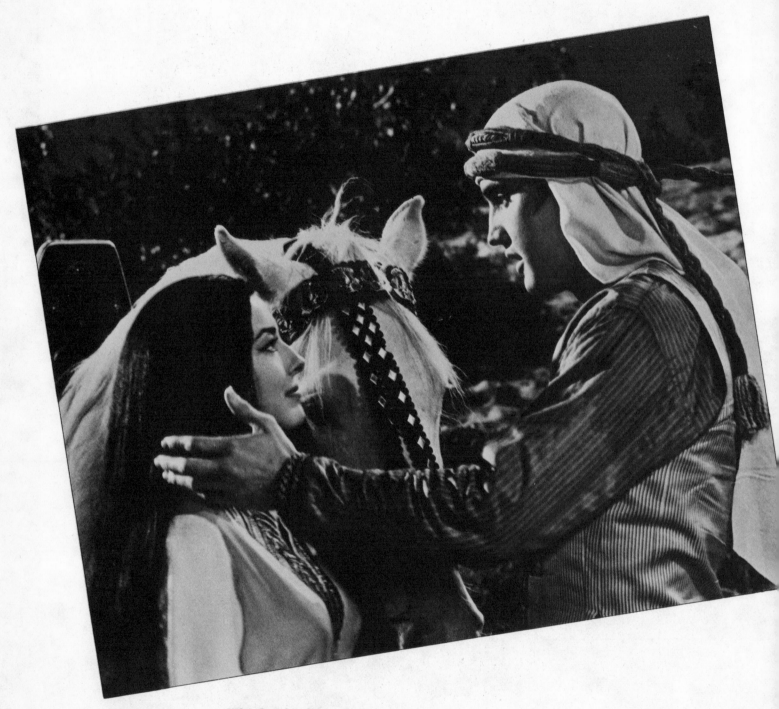

With Carolyn Carter
in **Harum Scarum**

Advertisement
for Harum
Scarum
(1965)

In **Harum Scarum**

In **Harum Scarum**

As the contemporary Rudolph Valentino in Harum Scarum

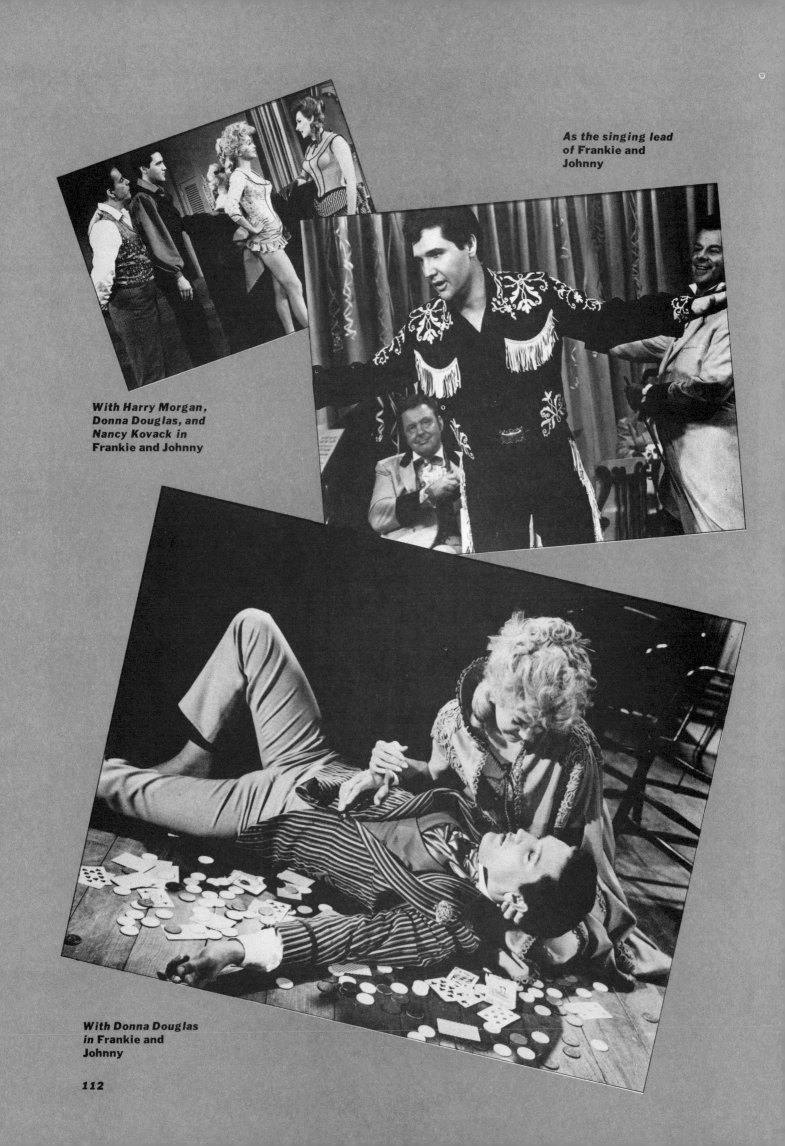

As the singing lead of Frankie and Johnny

With Harry Morgan, Donna Douglas, and Nancy Kovack *in* Frankie and Johnny

With Donna Douglas in Frankie and Johnny

112

Advertisement for Frankie and Johnny (1966)

With Donna Butterworth in *Paradise, Hawaiian Style*

In Paradise, Hawaiian Style

Advertisement for Paradise, Hawaiian Style (1966)

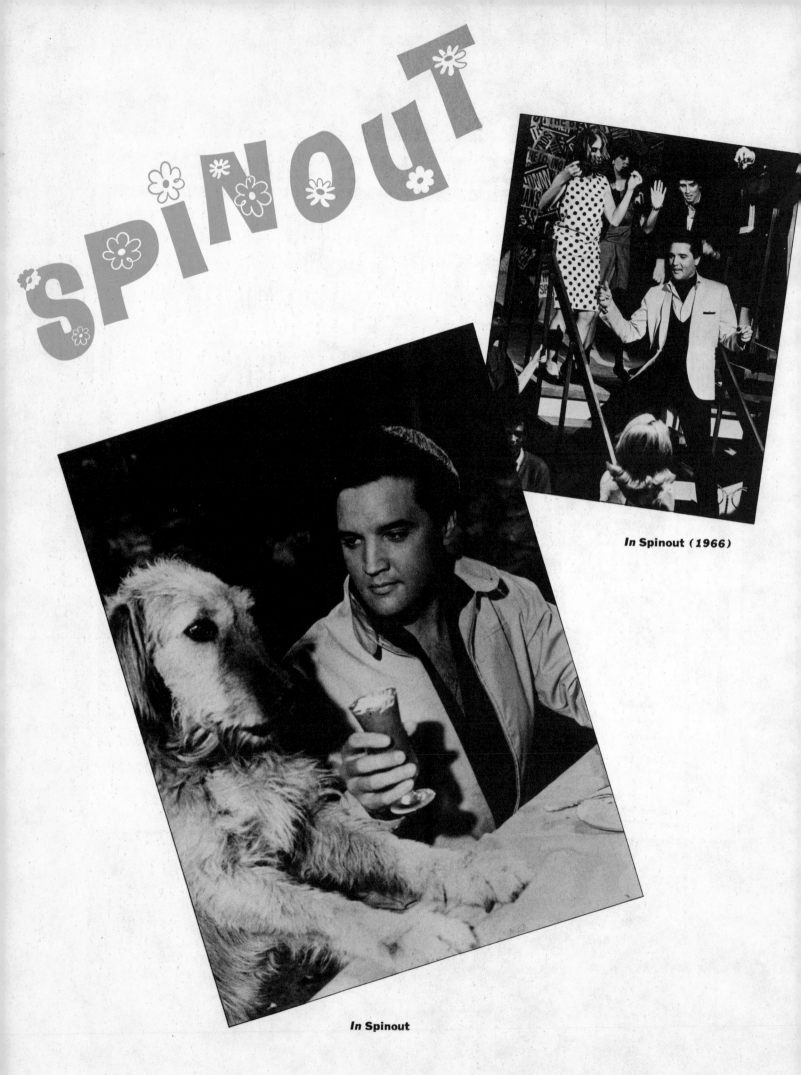

SPINOUT

In Spinout (1966)

In Spinout

**With Carl Betz,
Jimmy Hawkins,
Deborah Walley, and
Jack Mullaney in
Spinout**

**With Shelley
Fabares, Deborah
Walley, and Diane
McBain in Spinout**

Merchandising . . . .

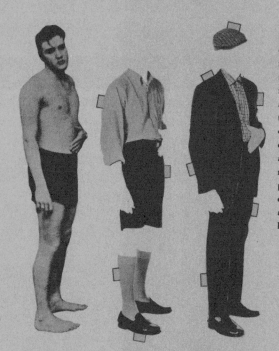

CUT-OUT DOLLS FOR GROWN-UP GIRLS

Urbane Elvis, man of distinction, mingles unnoticed with men of quality and affairs: the perfect choice to save embarrassment among diplomats, cosmopolitans and denizens of any city boulevard.

gates of Graceland locked, crashed angrily through the gate at seventy miles an hour in a Rolls-Royce limousine.

Elvis's temper tantrums were perhaps particularly difficult for his friends and family to deal with, because he'd always before been the polite, soft-spoken, and well-behaved "good boy" that his mother had brought him up to be in East Tupelo. (Of course, he'd been in a few well-publicized fist fights, in the early days, usually with some heckler who'd been riding him about his long hair or his pink jackets.) The di-

rectors of Elvis's movies, too, were constantly impressed at how easy he was to work with, his always saying "Yes, sir" to them and doing exactly as he was told to do. And musicians, engineers, and record-company executives who worked with him on recording sessions also invariably found him easy to get along with. And hard-working. But now, in the mid 1960s, as his career slumped, his waistline expanded, and his hair began to turn prematurely gray (he now dyes it black), he became increasingly temperamental and difficult to get along with.

Tupelo welcome for its most famous citizen

Kissing the bride

or years, Presley's name had been romantically linked (mainly by press agents) with one Hollywood starlet after another, from Ann-Margret to Kim Novak, Rita Moreno, Shelley Fabares, Judy Sprickles, and Suzanna Leigh. But, of course, he never married any of them, if, in fact, he actually ever dated any of them— Elvis has never been seen at a nightclub, in a restaurant, or at any Hollywood party other than his own. So his romantic life was basically a secret from the public.

While in Germany in the Army, however, Elvis had had a much-publicized romance with a fourteen-year-old American girl named Priscilla Beaulieu, who was the daughter of a U.S. Army major stationed in Frankfurt. Unknown to the public, who assumed that his fling with Priscilla had ended when he left Germany, Elvis had invited her back to America to spend Christmas, 1960, with him at Graceland. And he'd then talked her parents into letting Priscilla stay on and live at Graceland. Elvis's father, Vernon

Elvis and the former Priscilla Beaulieu being married in Las Vegas by Nevada Supreme Court Justice Davis Zenoff, May 1, 1967. The bride's sister, Michelle Beaulieu (right), is maid of honor.

had married again, to a woman he'd met in Germany named Dee Elliott, and so with Vernon and Dee as kind of surrogate parents, Priscilla moved into Graceland, enrolled in Memphis's Immaculate Conception High School, and saw Elvis only when he was back home between pictures. In June, 1963, Priscilla was graduated from high school, but she continued in the next years to live at Graceland while studying modeling and taking courses at a place called the Patricia Stevens Finishing and Career School.

In 1967, most of Elvis's fans assumed that he hadn't seen Priscilla in years. And so it came as a considerable surprise to them when—on May 1, 1967, in Las Vegas—he suddenly married Priscilla. They were married by a judge in a brief and simple ceremony that was followed, in the Aladdin Hotel, by a huge and garish reception staged by Colonel Parker mainly for the benefit of the press. The entire occasion, in fact, at a time when Elvis's career was seriously slipping, had the smell of an elaborate publicity

Examining the wedding ring

"With this ring, I thee wed."

Cutting the wedding cake

The proud parents preparing to leave Baptist Hospital in Memphis with their four-day-old daughter, Lisa Marie, born February 5, 1968

stunt. In any event, Priscilla and Elvis went off
to Palm Springs for a four-day honeymoon and
nine months later to the day, on February 1,
1968, had a child, a daughter whom they
named Lisa Marie.

Priscilla didn't at all get along with the rois-
tering members of the Memphis Mafia, and they
lost no love over her, either. But she won—all
but two of them were banished from Elvis's
entourage. In February, 1967, Elvis, whose

newest interest was horseback riding, had bought a 163-acre ranch about five miles south of Graceland (over the Mississippi border, in Walls) that he dubbed the Circle G. Costing him $250,000, the Circle G was a place where he could ride the stable of horses he'd bought, and it was at the Circle G, rather than at Graceland, that he lived with Priscilla and their infant daughter when they went home to Memphis. Meanwhile, he also bought a $400,000 mansion in the elegant Trousdale section of Los Angeles where he and Priscilla lived when they were in California.

By all accounts, including his own, Elvis never really settled down as a husband and father, and apparently most of the time totally ignored Priscilla and his child. Finally, in 1972, Priscilla simply took Lisa and walked out on Elvis. And on October 9, 1973, they were divorced. Amicably, as they say. Anyway, Priscilla got a settlement of $825,000 in cash, plus $6,000 a month for ten years, a 5-per-cent interest in a pair of music-publishing companies that Elvis owns, and $4,000 a month in child support. No wonder—from Priscilla's point of view, at least—the divorce was amicable. Today, Priscilla lives with Lisa in a $200,000 Los Angeles duplex apartment, co-owns a boutique for which she designs clothes, and never has a bad word to say to anyone about Elvis.

Elvis, Priscilla and Lisa, 1971

In the late 1960s, as a wave of nostalgia for the 1950s began to hit America, Elvis's singing career had a bit of an upturn. He did a fairly successful TV special in 1968 and in the winter of 1969 he had his first Number 1 record in seven years, "Suspicious Minds," which sold more than a million copies. And it was soon followed by "Don't Cry, Daddy," a Mac Davis ballad that—although it rose no higher than Number 6 in the charts— also sold a million copies. And he had substantial hits around that time, too, with "Kentucky Rain" and "In the Ghetto."

Meanwhile, however, Elvis's movie career had gone all to hell—audiences had simply stopped going to see his pictures. In the middle of the 1960s, when Elvis had been riding high in the movies and making a couple of million from each of them, Colonel Parker had foxily figured that they could make even more money from the pictures if they produced them for

**With Dodie Marshall
in** Easy Come, Easy
Go

In Easy Come, Easy
Go

**With Elsa Lanchester
in** Easy Come, Easy
Go

Advertisement for Easy Come, Easy Go (1967)

With Annette Day in Double Trouble

As singer Guy Lambert in Double Trouble

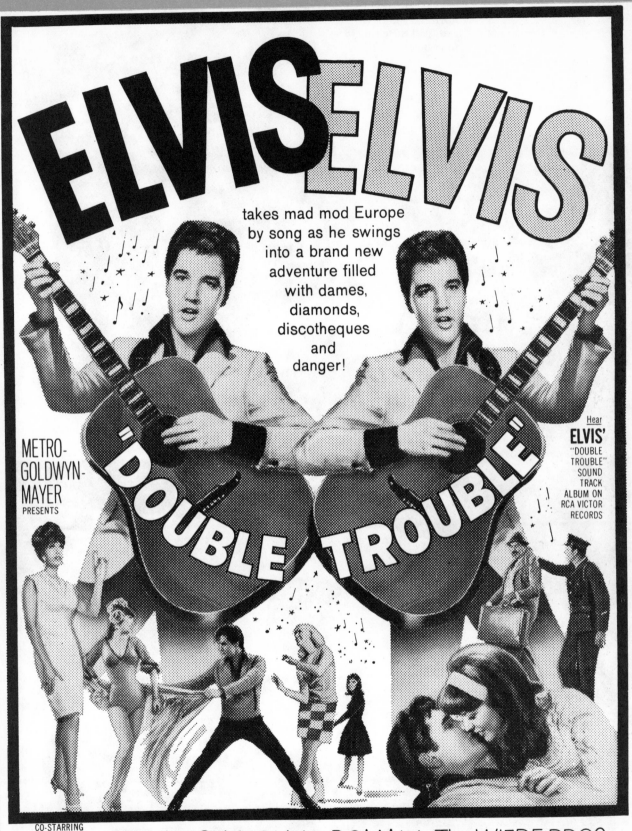

Advertisement for Double Trouble (1967)

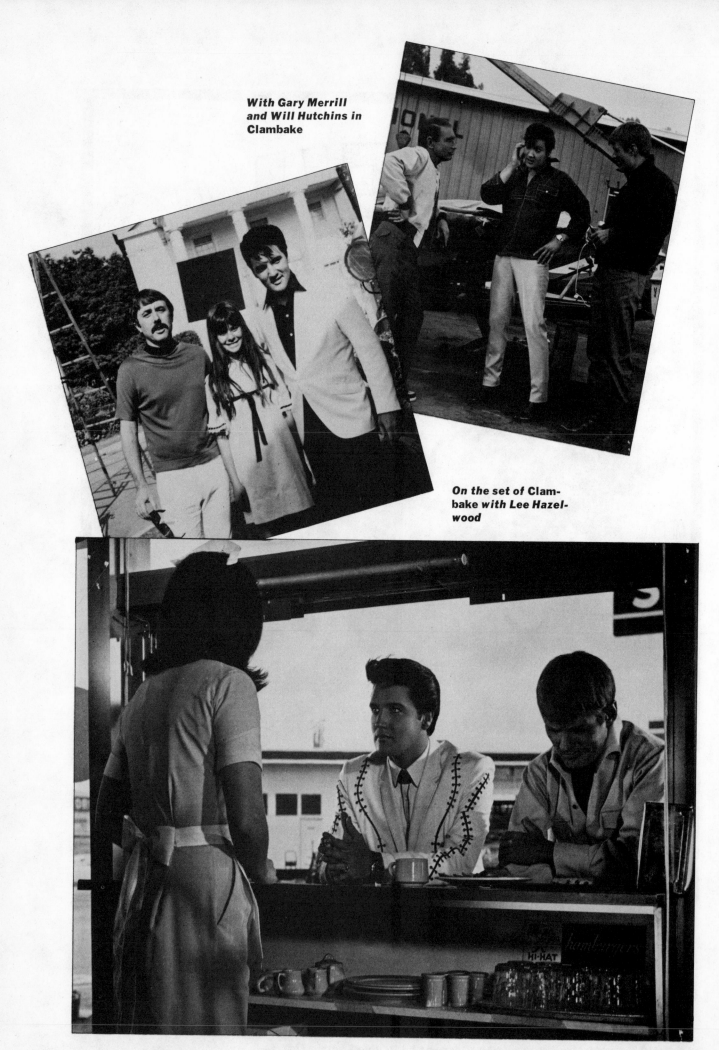

With Gary Merrill and Will Hutchins in Clambake

On the set of Clambake with Lee Hazelwood

With Will Hutchins in Clambake

132

Advertisement for Clambake (1967)

As Joe Lightcloud in
Stay Away, Joe

In Stay Away, Joe

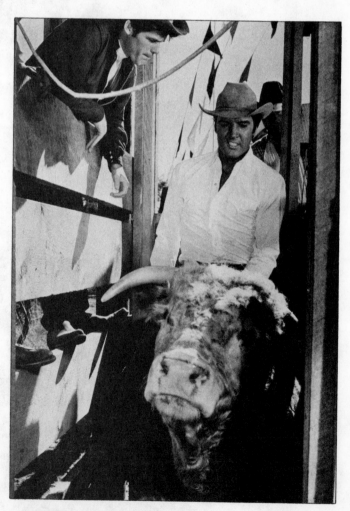

With Quentin Dean in
Stay Away, Joe

With Joan Blondell
in Stay Away, Joe

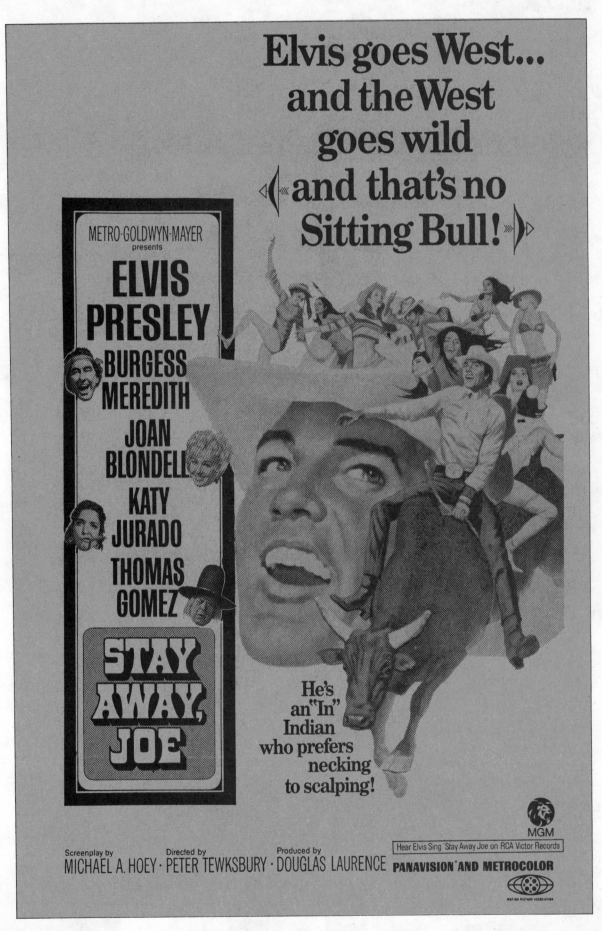

Advertisement for Stay Away, Joe (1968)

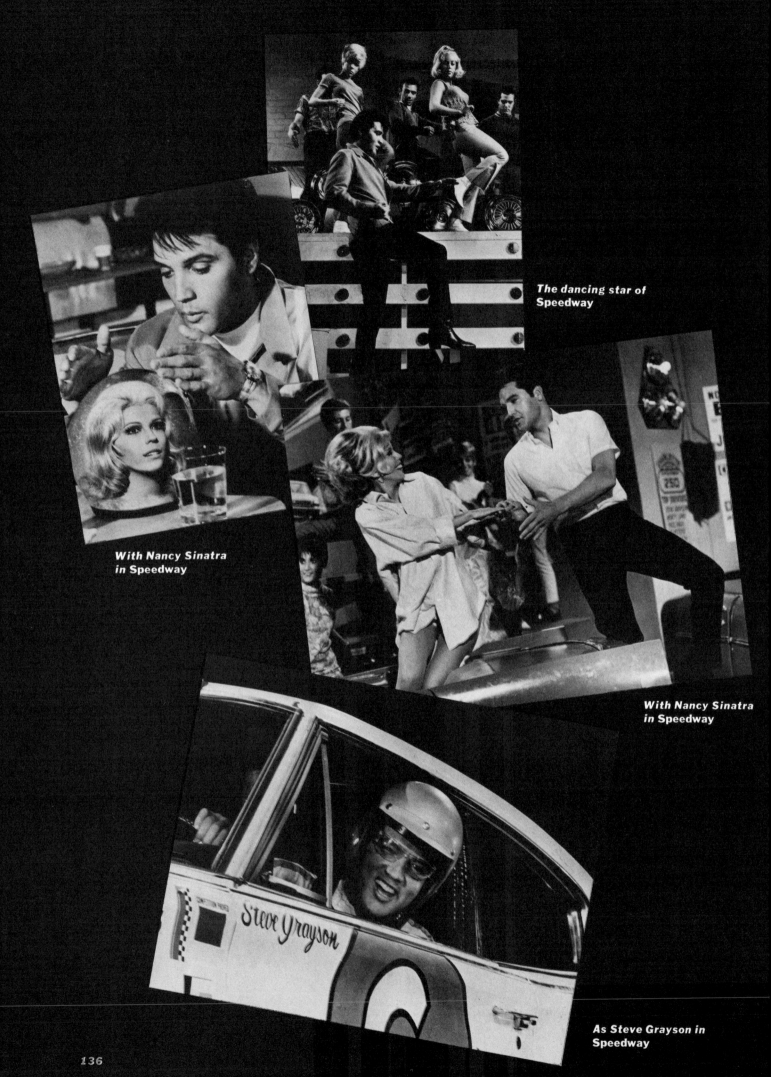

The dancing star of
Speedway

With Nancy Sinatra
in Speedway

With Nancy Sinatra
in Speedway

As Steve Grayson in
Speedway

Advertisement for Speedway (1968)

As photographer Greg in Live a Little, Love a Little

With Michele Carey in Live a Little, Love a Little

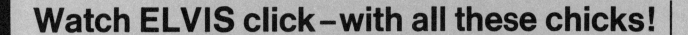

Watch ELVIS click—with all these chicks!

ELVIS shoots
the works
from dawn
to darkroom…
as a pin-up
photographer
who doesn't
want to get
pinned
down!

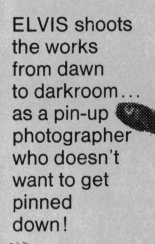

Hear **ELVIS** sing "Almost in Love"
and "A Little Less Conversation"
on RCA Records.

METRO-GOLDWYN-MAYER
PRESENTS
A DOUGLAS LAURENCE
PRODUCTION
STARRING

ELVIS PRESLEY
shows you how to
LIVE A LITTLE
LOVE A LITTLE

CO STARRING
MICHELE CAREY · DON PORTER · RUDY VALLEE · DICK SARGENT
SCREENPLAY BY
MICHAEL A. HOEY AND **DAN GREENBURG**   BASED O   LIPS" BY DAN GREENBURG
DIRECTED BY   PRODUCED BY
NORMAN TAUROG · DO   nd METROCOLOR   MGM

***Advertisement for
Live a Little, Love a
Little (1968)***

In **Live a Little, Love
a Little**

With Ina Balin in Charro

Promotional for Charro!

A DIFFERENT KIND OF ROLE.
A DIFFERENT KIND OF MAN.

*On his neck
he wore the
brand of a killer
On his hip he wore
vengeance.*

National General Pictures presents

ELVIS
PRESLEY
as **CHARRO!**

**Advertisement for
Charro! (1969)**

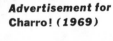

141

With Marlyn Mason in The Trouble with Girls

With Sheree North in The Trouble with Girls (1969)

THE TROUBLE WITH GIRLS

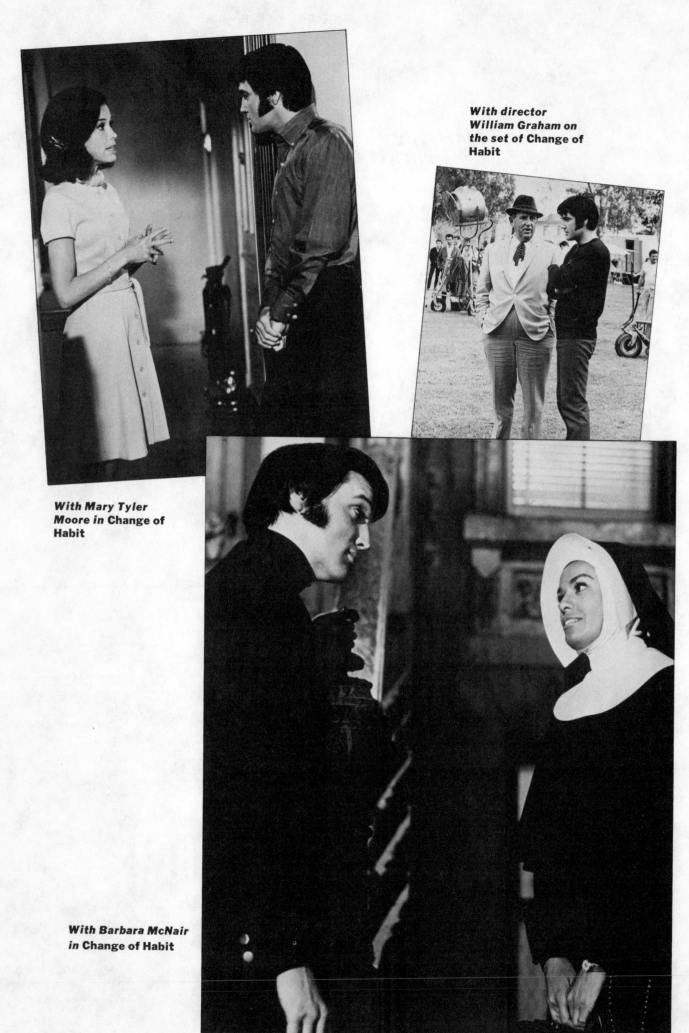

With director
William Graham on
the set of Change of
Habit

With Mary Tyler
Moore in Change of
Habit

With Barbara McNair
in Change of Habit

144

Could he make her
forget her vows and
follow her heart...

ELVIS PRESLEY
MARY TYLER MOORE
"CHANGE OF HABIT"
CO-STARRING
BARBARA McNAIR • **JANE ELLIOT** / Music by WILLIAM GOLDENBERG • Screenplay by
JAMES LEE & S. S. SCHWEITZER and ERIC

Advertisement for Change of Habit (1969)

less money. Previously, such Presley films as *Fun in Acapulco* had been budgeted at around $4 million. And so by the Hollywood rule of thumb that a film must gross 2½ times its cost before making a profit, no money was made on a picture like *Fun in Acapulco* until after it had grossed $10 million. And the shooting schedule for a picture like *Fun in Acapulco* or *Viva Las Vegas* was two months or more. But Colonel Parker now made a deal whereby Elvis's pictures would henceforth be produced by "Jungle Sam" Katzman, who was known around Hollywood as the "King of the Quickies." Thus, the first Katzman-produced Presley film, *Kissin' Cousins*, was made on a budget of $1.3 million and shot in seventeen days. The Colonel, who, astonishingly enough, claimed never even to have seen any of Elvis's movies, simply and rather arrogantly figured that Presley's fans would flock to the movies no matter how ineptly they were made. And, after all, a movie that cost $1.3 million to make would begin to show a profit after grossing only $3.25 million. But this time the Colonel may have at last outfoxed himself, because, as Elvis's pictures dropped in quality, the amount of money that they took in began to plummet. To the point where the movies were finally losing money instead of making it. Suddenly, Elvis was box-office poison and washed up in the movies. And now, except for a couple of feature-length documentaries about his doings (*Elvis: That's the Way It Is*, 1970, and *Elvis on Tour*, 1972), he hasn't made a movie since *Change of Habit*, a 1969 bomb in which he played a sensitive but misunderstood singing slum doctor opposite Mary Tyler Moore as the nun he falls in love with.

The collapse of Elvis's movie career was for the most part the fault of the Colonel, who, by the way, can be an extremely unpleasant man. Indeed, the Colonel's personal philosophy can be summed up in his own now-classic line: "You don't have to be nice to the people you meet on the way up if you're not coming back down again."

With Ina Balin in Charro

With his movie career in ruins, and his records selling only moderately well, Elvis turned in 1969 to playing Las Vegas. On July 31, 1969, appearing in public for the first time in seven years, he had a glittering and gala opening at Las Vegas's International Hotel. Billed as the "King of Rock 'n' Roll," he reverted to his raunchy 1956 style, knocking his middle-aged audience dead with driving renditions of "Blue Suede Shoes," "Hound Dog," and others of his earliest hits, sung complete with twitching legs and gyrating pelvis—although the old movements were done now for comic effect. Elvis played the International for a month, at a reported salary of $250,000 per week (only Sinatra and Barbra Streisand earn equal money in Las Vegas), and there wasn't an empty seat in the place during his entire engagement. At least in terms of being an in-person entertainer, Elvis was back on top.

Lovin' 'em tender once again

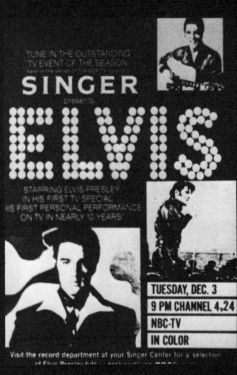

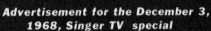
Advertisement for the December 3, 1968, Singer TV special

Elvis in action on the Singer show

Since 1969, Presley has regularly appeared twice a year in Las Vegas, for a month in the summer and another in the winter, at $1 million per engagement, and he's also each year made a national tour, packing them in in such enormous forums as the Houston Astrodome and New York's Madison Square Garden. Nowadays, however, there are few teen-agers in his audiences. Instead, most of those who come to see him are sedate housewives of thirty-five or so —the screaming teen-agers of 1956 grown older, who attend Elvis's concerts perhaps at least partially out of nostalgia for their lost 1950s youth. But, for whatever reason they pay to see him, Elvis remains today one of the most successful entertainers in America, earning around $5 million a year even though he's neither made a movie nor had a hit record in years.

When Priscilla moved out on Elvis, in 1972, the Memphis Mafia immediately moved back in, and Elvis and his buddies once again resumed their fraternity-house life of round-the-clock parties and horseplay. And soon, too, Elvis

There's more than one way to play a guitar!

A thoughtful moment in a busy day

again found himself with a serious weight problem. By the summer of 1974, in fact, he'd bloated up to 240 pounds—when he appeared in Las Vegas, no photographs were allowed to be taken of him, and anyone who tried to had his camera busted by the Memphis Mafia. The Las Vegas audiences were not only appalled at his chubbiness; they also complained that he was no longer giving his all on stage, but was instead mumbling his way through his songs and spending half of his act bickering with some of the onlookers. Explain his friends: "Elvis is exhausted and worn out from too much performing. He used to love it, but now it's an ordeal for him to get through a performance."

On January 8, 1975, Elvis Presley celebrated his fortieth birthday. But it was far from a gala occasion. Instead, on a crash diet that was supposedly designed to get him back down to 180 pounds, he spent the day moping alone in his bedroom at Graceland. A week and a half after that, at 4:00 A.M. on the morning of January 20,

CASINO LOUNGE
THE 'BOSS of the BLUES' IS BACK!
B. B. KING
QUANTRELL

LAS VEGAS HILTON
ELVIS
JACKIE KAHANE   SWEET INSPIRATIONS
J.D. SUMNER and the STAMPS QUARTET
MUSICAL DIRECTION   JOE GUERCIO

BACCARAT AROUND THE CLOCK

DINE TONIGHT
IN ONE OF OUR
FIVE   UNUSUAL
FOREIGN
RESTAURANTS

News conference following opening at Las Vegas International

Arriving for the wedding of Delbert B. ("Sonny") West, his chief security officer, Memphis, December 29, 1970

At Las Vegas International Hotel, August 1970

Performing in Las Vegas, 1969

In **Elvis That's the Way It Is** *(1970)*

Elvis on Tour (1972)

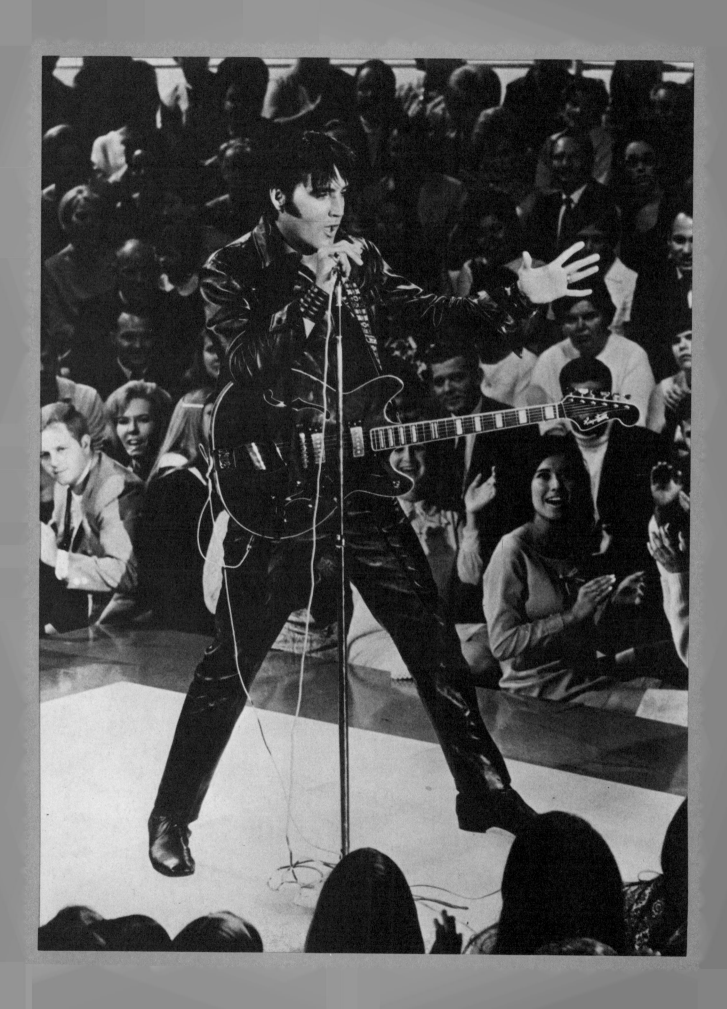

. . . . I'm all shook up"

With Lamar Fike, Sonny West, Joe Esposito, and the
Colonel at Virginia airport, 1972

Recording session

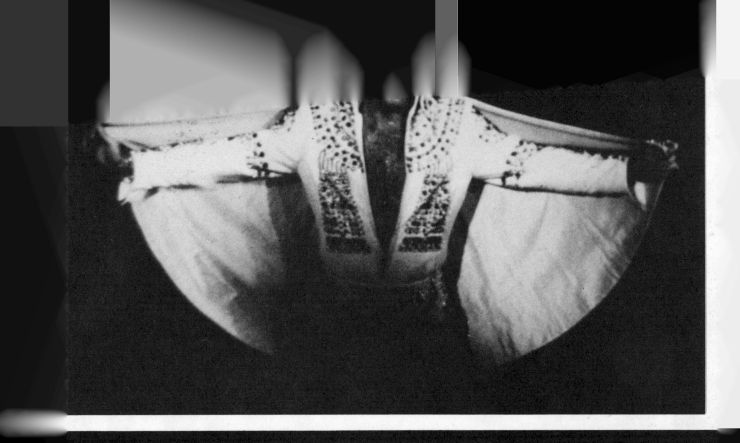

At Nassau Coliseum, Long Island, 1973

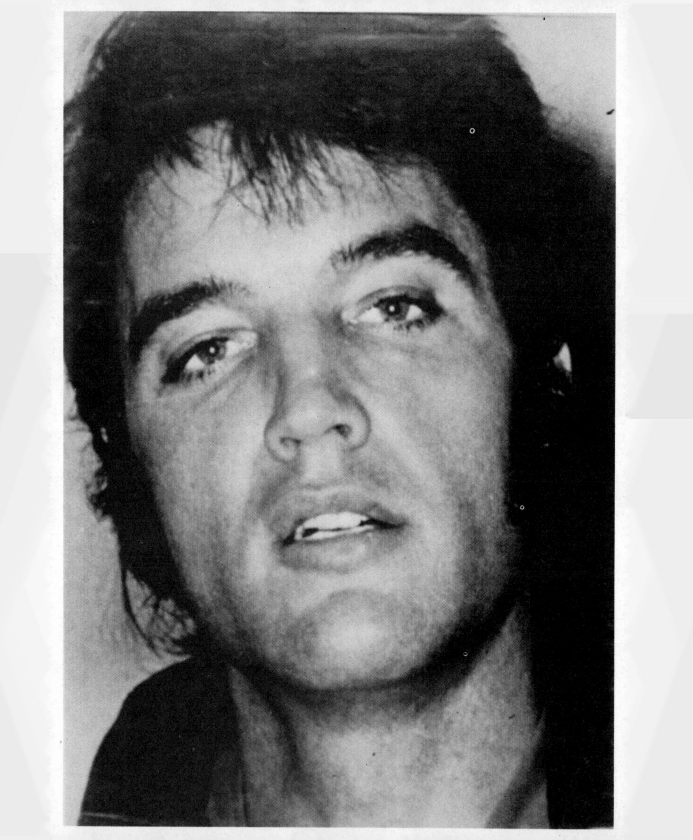

1975, he was rushed to a hospital in Memphis with what was later described as a "blockage of the colon." Once again, he'd been overeating and gaining weight, and the Memphis doctors put him on an all-liquid diet for four weeks. And told him, when he left the hospital, on February 13, to eat more reasonably and to get himself some exercise.

But, age and overweight notwithstanding, Elvis is still very much the "King of Rock 'n' Roll." And no matter what happens in the future, he's already had one of the most astonishingly successful careers in the history of American show business. Not even he knows how to explain his success. "I don't know what it is—I just fell into it, really," Elvis told an interviewer a while ago. "I remember my daddy and me talkin' about it years ago. Laughin'. He looked at me and said, 'What happened, El? The last thing I remember is I was working in a paint factory and you was driving a truck.' And I remember how, after something big happened along about 1957, I was sittin' at home and found my mama staring at me. I asked her why and she just shook her head and said, 'I don't believe it. I just don't believe it.' And I guess I feel that same way about it still. It just . . . caught me up."

Elvis, 1974

Elvis Presley Discography

Singles

SUN RECORDS

August 1954   *That's All Right (Mama)/Blue Moon of Kentucky*
SUN 209

October 1954   *Good Rockin' Tonight/I Don't Care if the Sun Don't Shine*
SUN 210

January 1955   *Milkcow Blues Boogie/You're a Heartbreaker*
SUN 215

May 1955   *I'm Left, You're Right, She's Gone/Baby, Let's Play House*
SUN 217

August 1955   *Mystery Train/I Forgot to Remember to Forget*
SUN 223

RCA VICTOR

November 1955   *Mystery Train/I Forgot to Remember to Forget*
RCA 6357

November 1955   *That's All Right (Mama)/Blue Moon of Kentucky*
RCA 6380

November 1955   *Good Rockin' Tonight/I Don't Care if the Sun Don't Shine*
RCA 6381

November 1955   *Milkcow Blues Boogie/You're a Heartbreaker*
RCA 6382

November 1955   *I'm Left, You're Right, She's Gone/Baby Let's Play House*
RCA 6383

January 1956   *Heartbreak Hotel/I Was the One*
RCA 6420

May 1956   *I Want You, I Need You, I Love You/My Baby Left Me*
RCA 6540

July 1956   *Hound Dog/Don't Be Cruel*
RCA 6604

| September 1956 | Blue Suede Shoes/Tutti Frutti |
| | RCA 6636 |

| September 1956 | I'm Counting on You/I Got a Woman |
| | RCA 6637 |

September 1956   I'll Never Let You Go/I'm Gonna Sit Right Down and Cry Over You
RCA 6638

September 1956   Tryin' to Get to You/I Love You Because
RCA 6639

September 1956   Blue Moon/Just Because
RCA 6640

September 1956   Money Honey/One-Sided Love Affair
RCA 6641

September 1956   Shake, Rattle and Roll/Lawdy, Miss Clawdy
RCA 6642

September 1956   Love Me Tender/Any Way You Want Me
RCA 6643

January 1957   Too Much/Playing for Keeps
RCA 6800

March 1957   All Shook Up/That's When Your Heartaches Begin
RCA 6870

June 1957   Teddy Bear/Loving You
RCA 7000

September 1957   Jailhouse Rock/Treat Me Nice
RCA 7035

December 1957   Don't/I Beg of You
RCA 7150

April 1958   Wear My Ring Around Your Neck/Doncha' Think It's Time
RCA 7240

June 1958   Hard Headed Woman/Don't Ask Me Why
RCA 7280

October 1958   I Got Stung/One Night
RCA 7410

March 1959   A Fool Such As I/I Need Your Love Tonight
RCA 7506

June 1959   A Big Hunk o' Love/My Wish Came True
RCA 7600

March 1960   Stuck on You/Fame and Fortune
RCA 7740

July 1960 *It's Now or Never/A Mess of Blues*
         RCA 7777

November 1960 *Are You Lonesome Tonight/I Gotta Know*
           RCA 7810

February 1961 *Surrender/Lonely Man*
        RCA 7850

May 1961 *I Feel So Bad/Wild in the Country*
        RCA 7880

August 1961 *Little Sister/His Latest Flame*
        RCA 7908

November 1961 *Can't Help Falling in Love/Rock-a-Hula Baby*
          RCA 7968

February 1962 *Good Luck Charm/Anything That's Part of You*
          RCA 7992

July 1962 *She's Not You/Just Tell Her Jim Said Hello*
        RCA 8041

October 1962 *Return to Sender/Where Do You Come From*
        RCA 8100

January 1963 *One Broken Heart for Sale/They Remind Me Too Much of You*
          RCA 8134

June 1963 *(You're the) Devil in Disguise/Please Don't Drag That String Around*
          RCA 8188

October 1963 *Bossa Nova Baby/Witcher*
        RCA 8243

October 1963 *Kissin' Cousins/It Hurts Me*
        RCA 8307

April 1964 *Kiss Me Quick/Suspicion*
        RCA 0639

April 1964 *Viva Las Vegas/What'd I Say*
        RCA 8360

July 1964 *Such a Night/Never Ending*
        RCA 8400

September 1964 *Ain't that Loving You, Baby/Ask Me*
          RCA 8440

November 1964 *Blue Christmas/Wooden Heart*
        RCA 0720

March 1965 *Do the Clam/You'll Be Gone*
        RCA 8500

April 1965   *Crying in the Chapel/I Believe in the Man in the Sky*
                                                    RCA 0643

May 1965   *(Such an) Easy Question/It Feels So Right*
                                                    RCA 8585

August 1965   *I'm Yours/(It's a) Long Lonely Highway*
                                                    RCA 8657

October 1965   *Puppet on a String/Wooden Heart*
                                                    RCA 0650

November 1965   *Blue Christmas/Santa Claus Is Back in Town*
                                                    RCA 0647

January 1966   *Tell Me Why/Blue River*
                                                    RCA 8740

February 1966   *Joshua Fit the Battle/Known Only to Him*
                                                    RCA 0651

February 1966   *Milky White Way/Swing Down Sweet Chariot*
                                                    RCA 0652

March 1966   *Frankie and Johnny/Please Don't Stop Loving Me*
                                                    RCA 8780

June 1966   *Love Letters/Come What May*
                                                    RCA 8870

October 1966   *Spinout/All that I Am*
                                                    RCA 8941

November 1966   *If Every Day Was Like Christmas/How Would You Like To Be*
                                                    RCA 8950

January 1967   *Indescribably Blue/Fools Fall in Love*
                                                    RCA 9056

May 1967   *Long Legged Girl (with the Short Dress On)/That's Someone You Never Forget*
                                                    RCA 9115

August 1967   *There's Always Me/Judy*
                                                    RCA 9287

September 1967   *Big Boss Man/You Don't Know Me*
                                                    RCA 9341

January 1968   *Guitar Man/High Heel Sneakers*
                                                    RCA 9425

March 1968   *U.S. Male/Stay Away, Joe*
                                                    RCA 9465

April 1968   *You'll Never Walk Alone/We Call on Him*
                                                    RCA 9600

May 1968   *Let Yourself Go/Your Time Hasn't Come Yet, Baby*
RCA 9547

September 1968   *A Little Less Conversation/Almost in Love*
RCA 9610

October 1968   *If I Can Dream/Edge of Reality*
RCA 9670

March 1969   *Memories/Charro*
RCA 9731

April 1969   *How Great Thou Art/His Hand in Mine*
RCA 0130

April 1969   *In the Ghetto/Any Day Now*
RCA 9741

June 1969   *Clean Up Your Own Back Yard/The Fair Is Moving On*
RCA 9747

August 1969   *Suspicious Minds/You'll Think of Me*
RCA 9764

November 1969   *Don't Cry, Daddy/Rubberneckin'*
RCA 9768

January 1970   *Kentucky Rain/My Little Friend*
RCA 9791

May 1970   *The Wonder of You/Mama Liked the Roses*
RCA 9835

July 1970   *I've Lost You/The Next Step Is Love*
RCA 9873

October 1970   *You Don't Have to Say You Love Me/Patch It up*
RCA 9916

December 1970   *Rags to Riches/Where Did They Go Lord*
RCA 9980

March 1971   *I Really Don't Want to Know/There Goes My Everything*
RCA 9960

May 1971   *Life/Only Believe*
RCA 9985

August 1971   *I'm Leavin'/Heart of Rome*
RCA 9998

October 1971   *It's Only Love/The Sound of Your Cry*
RCA 1017

November 1971   *Merry Christmas Baby/O Come All Ye Faithful*
RCA 0572

January 1972   *Until It's Time for You to Go/We Can Make the Morning*
RCA 0619

March 1972   *He Touched Me/Bosom of Abraham*
RCA 0651

April 1972   *An American Trilogy/The First Time Ever I Saw Your Face*
RCA 0672

September 1972   *Burning Love/It's a Matter of Time*
RCA 0769

November 1972   *Separate Ways/Always on My Mind*
RCA 0815

February 1973   *Fool/Steamroller Blues*
RCA 0910

September 1973   *Raised on Rock/For Ol' Times Sake*
RCA 0088

February 1974   *Take Good Care of Her/I've Got a Thing about You Baby*
RCA 0196

June 1974   *Help Me/If You Talk in Your Sleep*
RCA 0280

October 1974   *It's Midnight/Promised Land*
RCA 10074

February 1975   *My Boy/Thinking about You*
RCA 10191

45 rpm Extended Play (EP) Albums

R.C.A.

1956   Elvis Presley, Vol. 1
Blue Suede Shoes, I'm Counting on You, I Got a Woman, One-Sided Love Affair
RCA EPA 747

1956   Elvis Presley, Vol. 2
Tutti Frutti, Tryin' to Get to You, I'm Gonna Sit Right Down and Cry,
I'll Never Let You Go
RCA EPA 1254

1956   Heartbreak Hotel
Heartbreak Hotel, I Was the One, I Forgot to Remember to Forget, Money Honey
RCA EPA 821

1956   Elvis Presley
        Shake, Rattle and Roll, I Love You Because, Blue Moon, Lawdy, Miss Clawdy
                                                            RCA EPA 830

1956   The Real Elvis
        Don't Be Cruel, I Want You, I Need You, I Love You, Hound Dog, My Baby Left Me
                                                            RCA EPA 940

1956   Any Way You Want Me
        Any Way You Want Me, I'm Left, You're Right, She's Gone, I Don't Care if the
        Sun Don't Shine, Mystery Train   RCA EPA 965

1956   Love Me Tender
        Love Me Tender, Let Me Be, Poor Boy, We're Gonna Move   RCA EPA 4006

1956   Elvis, Vol. 1
        Rip It Up, Love Me, When My Blue Moon Turns to Gold Again, Paralyzed
                                                            RCA EPA 992

1956   Elvis, Vol. 2
        So Glad You're Mine, Old Shep, Ready Teddy, Anyplace Is Paradise   RCA EPA 993

1957   Strictly Elvis
        Long Tall Sally, First in Line, How Do You Think I Feel,
        How's the World Treating You   RCA EPA 994

1957   Loving You, Vol. 1
        Loving You, Party, Teddy Bear, True Love   RCA EPA 1-1515

1957   Loving You, Vol. 2
        Lonesome Cowboy, Hot Dog, Mean Woman Blues, Got a Lot o' Livin' to Do
                                                            RCA EPA 2-1515

1957   Just for You
        I Need You So, Have I Told You Lately That I Love You, Blueberry Hill,
        Is It So Strange   RCA EPA 4041

1957   Peace in the Valley
        Peace in the Valley, It Is No Secret, I Believe, Take My Hand, Precious Lord
                                                            RCA EPA 4054

1957   Elvis Sings Christmas Songs
        Santa Bring My Baby Back, Blue Christmas, Santa Claus Is Back In Town,
        I'll Be Home for Christmas   RCA EPA 4108

1957   Jailhouse Rock
        Jailhouse Rock, Young and Beautiful, I Want to Be Free, Don't Leave Me Now,
        Baby, I Don't Care   RCA EPA 4114

| 1958 | *King Creole, New Orleans, As Long As I Have You, Lover Doll* | RCA EPA 4319 |

1958   King Creole, Vol. 2
Trouble, Young Dreams, Crawfish, Dixieland Rock   RCA EPA 4321

1958   Elvis Sails
Press interview with Elvis Presley at the Brooklyn Army Terminal
(September 22, 1958)   RCA EPA 4325

1958   Christmas with Elvis
White Christmas, Here Comes Santa Claus, O Little Town of Bethlehem,
Silent Night   RCA EPA 4340

1959   A Touch of Gold, Vol. 1
Hard Headed Woman, Good Rockin' Tonight, Don't, I Beg of You   RCA EPA 5088

1959   A Touch of Gold, Vol. 2
Wear My Ring Around Your Neck, Treat Me Nice, One Night,
That's All Right (Mama)   RCA EPA 5101

1960   A Touch of Gold, Vol. 3
Blue Moon of Kentucky, All Shook Up, Don't Ask Me Why, Too Much   RCA EPA 5141

1962   Follow that Dream
Follow that Dream, What a Wonderful Life, Angel, I'm Not the Marrying Kind
  RCA EPA 4368

1962   Kid Galahad
This Is Living, I Got Lucky, A Whistling Tune, King of the Whole Wide World,
Riding the Rainbow, Home Is Where the Heart Is   RCA EPA 4371

1964   Viva Las Vegas
If You Think I Don't Need You, I Need Somebody to Lean On, C'mon Everybody,
Tomorrow and Forever   RCA EPA 4382

1965   Tickle Me
I Feel that I've Known You Forever, Slowly But Surely, Night Rider, Dirty,
Dirty Feeling, Put the Blame on Me   RCA EPA 4383

1967   Easy Come, Easy Go
Easy Come, Easy Go, The Love Machine, Yoga Is As Yoga Does, You Gotta Stop,
Sing, You Children, I'll Take Love   RCA EPA 4387

Albums

R.C.A.

April
1956   Elvis Presley
Blue Suede Shoes, I'm Counting on You, I Got a Woman, One-Sided Love Affair, I Love You Because, Just Because, Tutti Frutti, Tryin' to Get to You, I'm Gonna Sit Right Down and Cry, I'll Never Let You Go, Blue Moon, Money Honey
RCA LSP 1254

October
1956   Elvis
Rip It Up, Love Me, When My Blue Moon Turns to Gold Again, Long Tall Sally, First in Line, Paralyzed, So Glad You're Mine, Old Shep, Ready Teddy, Anyplace Is Paradise, How's the World Treating You, How Do You Think I Feel   RCA LSP 1382

July
1957   Loving You
From the film: Mean Woman Blues, Teddy Bear, Loving You, Got A Lot o' Lovin' to Do, Lonesome Cowboy, Hot Dog, Party, Bonus Songs: Blueberry Hill, True Love, Don't Leave Me Now, Have I Told You Lately That I Love You, I Need You So
RCA LSP 1515

November
1957   Elvis' Christmas Album
Santa Claus Is Back in Town, White Christmas, Here Comes Santa Claus, I'll Be Home for Christmas, Blue Christmas, Santa Bring My Baby Back, O Little Town of Bethlehem, Silent Night, Peace in the Valley, Believe, Take My Hand, Precious Lord, It Is No Secret   RCA LSP 1035

March
1958   Elvis' Golden Records
Hound Dog, Loving You, All Shook Up, Heartbreak Hotel, Jailhouse Rock, Love Me, Too Much, Don't Be Cruel, That's When Your Heartaches Begin, Teddy Bear, Love Me Tender, Treat Me Nice, Any Way You Want Me, I Want You, I Need You, I Love You   RCA LSP 1707

August
1958   King Creole
King Creole, As Long As I Have You, Hard Headed Woman, Trouble, Dixieland Rock, Don't Ask Me Why, Lover Doll, Crawfish, Young Dreams, Steadfast, Loyal and True, New Orleans   RCA LSP 1884

February
1959   For LP Fans Only
*That's All Right, Lawdy, Miss Clawdy, Mystery Train, Poor Boy, Playing for
Keeps, My Baby Left Me, I Was the One, Shake, Rattle and Roll, You're a
Heartbreaker, I'm Left, You're Right, She's Gone*   RCA LSP 1990

August
1959   A Date with Elvis
*Blue Moon of Kentucky, Young and Beautiful, Baby, I Don't Care, Milkcow Blues
Boogie, Baby, Let's Play House, Good Rockin' Tonight, Is It So Strange, We're
Gonna Move, I Want to Be Free, I Forgot to Remember to Forget*   RCA LSP 2011

December
1959   50,000,000 Elvis Fans Can't Be Wrong
Elvis' Gold Records, Vol. 2
*A Fool Such As I, I Need Your Love Tonight, Wear My Ring Around Your Neck,
Doncha' Think It's Time, I Beg of You, A Big Hunk o' Love, Don't, My Wish Came
True, One Night, I Got Stung*   RCA LSP 2075

April
1960   Elvis Is Back
*Fever, Girl Next Door Went-A-Walking, Soldier Boy, Make Me Know It, I Will Be
Home Again, Reconsider, Baby, It Feels So Right, Like a Baby, The Girl of My
Best Friend, Thrill of Your Love, Such a Night, Dirty, Dirty Feeling*   RCA LSP 2231

October
1960   G. I. Blues
*Tonight Is So Right For Love, What's She Really Like, Frankfurt Special, Wooden
Heart, G.I. Blues, Pocketful of Rainbows, Shoppin' Around, Big Boots, Didja'
Ever, Blue Suede Shoes, Doin' the Best I Can*   RCA LSP 2256

December
1960   His Hand in Mine
*His Hand In Mine, I'm Gonna Walk Dem Golden Stairs, In My Father's House,
Milky White Way, Known Only to Him, I Believe in the Man in the Sky, Joshua Fit
the Battle, Jesus Knows What I Need, Swing Down, Sweet Chariot, Mansion
over the Hilltop, If We Never Meet Again, Working on the Building*   RCA LSP 2328

June
1961   Something for Everybody
*The Ballad Side: There's Always Me, Give Me the Right, It's a Sin, Sentimental
Me, Starting Today, Gently, The Rhythm Side: I'm Comin' Home, In Your Arms,
Put the Blame on Me, Judy, I Want You with Me; Bonus Songs: I Slipped, I Stumbled,
I Fell (from* Wild in the Country)   RCA LSP 2370

October
1961   Blue Hawaii
        *Blue Hawaii, Almost Always True, Aloha Oe, No More, Can't Help Falling in Love,
        Rock-a-Hula Baby, Moonlight Swim, Ku-u-i-po, Ito Eats, Slicin' Sand, Hawaiian
        Wedding Song*   RCA LSP 2436

June
1962   Pot Luck
        *Kiss Me Quick, Just for Old Times' Sake, Gonna Get Back Home Somehow, Easy
        Question, Steppin' Out of Line (from* Blue Hawaii*), I'm Yours, Something Blue,
        Suspicion, I Feel That I've Known You Forever, Night Rider, Fountain of Love,
        That's Someone You Never Forget*   RCA LSP 2523

November
1962   Girls! Girls! Girls!
        *Girls! Girls! Girls!, I Don't Wanna Be Tied, Where Do You Come From, I Don't
        Want To, We'll Be Together, A Boy Like Me, a Girl Like You, Earth Boy, Return to
        Sender, Because of Love, Thanks to the Rolling Sea, Song of the Shrimp, The
        Walls Have Ears, We're Coming in Loaded*   RCA LSP 2621

March
1963   It Happened at the World's Fair
        *Beyond the Bend, Relax, Take Me to the Fair, They Remind Me Too Much of You,
        One Broken Heart for Sale, I'm Falling in Love Tonight, Cotton Candy Land,
        A World of Our Own, How Would You Like to Be, Happy Ending*   RCA LSP 2697

September
1963   Elvis' Golden Records, Vol. 3
        *It's Now or Never, Stuck on You, Fame and Fortune, I Gotta Know, Surrender,
        I Feel So Bad, Are You Lonesome Tonight, His Latest Flame, Little Sister,
        Good Luck Charm, Anything That's Part of You, She's Not You*   RCA LSP 2765

November
1963   Fun in Acapulco
        *Fun in Acapulco, Vino, Dinero y Amor, Mexico, El Toro, Marguerita, The
        Bullfighter Was a Lady, No Room to Rhumba in a Sports Car, I Think I'm Gonna
        Like It Here, Bossa Nova Baby, You Can't Say No in Acapulco, Guadalajara;
        Bonus Songs: Love Me Tonight, Slowly But Surely*   RCA LSP 2756

March
1964   Kissin' Cousins
        *Kissin' Cousins, Smokey Mountain Boy, There's Gold in the Mountains, One Boy,
        Two Little Girls, Catchin' On Fast, Tender Feeling, Anyone, Barefoot Ballad,
        Once Is Enough; Bonus Songs: Echoes of Love, Long, Lonely Highway* RCA LSP 2894

October
1964   Roustabout
                *Roustabout, Little Egypt, Poison Ivy League, Hard Knocks, It's a Wonderful
                World, Big Love, Big Heartache, One-Track Heart, It's Carnival Time, Carny
                Town, There's a Brand New Day on the Horizon, Wheels on My Heels*   RCA LSP 2999

April
1965   Girl Happy
                *Girl Happy, Spring Fever, Fort Lauderdale Chamber of Commerce, Startin'
                Tonight, Wolf Call, Do Not Disturb, Cross My Heart and Hope to Die, The
                Meanest Girl in Town, Do the Clam, Puppet on a String, I've Got to Find My Baby;
                Bonus Song: You'll Be Gone*   RCA LSP 3338

July
1965   Elvis for Everyone
                *Your Cheatin' Heart, Summer Kisses, Winter Tears, Finders Keepers, Losers
                Weepers, In My Way (from* Wild in the Country*), Tomorrow Night, Memphis,
                Tennessee, For the Millionth and the Last Time, Forget Me Never (from* Wild in
                the Country*), Sound Advice (from* Follow That Dream*), Santa Lucia (from* Viva
                Las Vegas*), I Met Her Today, When It Rains, It Really Pours*   RCA LSP 3450

October
1965   Harum Scarum
                *Harem Holiday, My Desert Serenade, Go East—Young Man, Mirage, Kismet,
                Shake That Tambourine, Hey Little Girl, Golden Coins, So Close, Yet So Far;
                Bonus Songs: Animal Instinct, Wisdom of the Ages*   RCA LSP 3468

April
1966   Frankie and Johnny
                *Frankie and Johnny, Come Along, Petunia, the Gardener's Daughter, Chesay,
                What Every Woman Lives For, Look Out, Broadway, Beginner's Luck, Down by
                the Riverside and When the Saints Go Marching In (medley), Shout It Out,
                Hard Luck, Please Don't Stop Loving Me, Everybody Come Aboard*   RCA LSP 3553

June
1966   Paradise; Hawaiian Style
                *Paradise; Hawaiian Style, Queenie Wahine's Papaya, Scratch My Back, Drums of
                the Islands, Datin', A Dog's Life, House of Sand, Stop Where You Are, This Is My
                Heaven; Bonus Song: Sand Castles*   RCA LSP 3643

October
1966   Spinout
                *Stop, Look and Listen, Adam and Evil, All That I Am, Never Say Yes, Am I Ready,
                Beach Shack, Spinout, Smorgasbord, I'll Be Back; Bonus Songs: Tomorrow Is a
                Long Time, Down in the Alley, I'll Remember You*   RCA LSP 3702

March
1967   How Great Thou Art
How Great Thou Art, In the Garden, Somebody Bigger Than You and I, Farther Along, Stand by Me, Without Him, So High, Where Could I Go But to the Lord, By and By, If the Lord Wasn't Walking by My Side, Run On, Where No One Stands Alone, Crying in the Chapel   RCA LSP 3758

June
1967   Double Trouble
Double Trouble, Baby, If You'll Give Me All of Your Love, Could I Fall in Love, Long Legged Girl, City by Night, Old MacDonald, I Love Only One Girl, There Is So Much World to See; Bonus Songs: *It Won't Be Long, Never Ending, Blue River, What Now, What Next, Where To*   RCA LSP 3787

November
1967   Clambake
Clambake, Who Needs Money, A House That Has Everything, Confidence, Hey, Hey, Hey, You Don't Know Me, The Girl I Never Loved; Bonus Songs: *Guitar Man, How Can You Lose What You Never Had, Big Boss Man, Singing Tree, Just Call Me Lonesome*   RCA LSP 3893

February
1968   Elvis' Gold Records, Vol. 4
Love Letters, Witchcraft, It Hurts Me, What'd I Say, Please Don't Drag That String Around, Indescribably Blue, You're the Devil in Disguise, Lonely Man, A Mess of Blues, Ask Me, Ain't That Loving You, Baby, Just Tell Her Jim Said Hello   RCA LSP 3921

June
1968   Speedway
Speedway, There Ain't Nothing Like a Song (with Nancy Sinatra), *Your Time Hasn't Come Yet Baby, Who Are You, He's Your Uncle, Not Your Dad, Let Yourself Go, Your Groovy Self* (with Nancy Sinatra); Bonus Songs: *Five Sleepy Heads, Western Union, Mine, Goin' Home, Suppose*   RCA LSP 3989

November
1968   Elvis Singing Flaming Star and Others
Flaming Star (from Flaming Star), *Wonderful World (from* Live a Little, Love a Little), *Night Life, All I Needed Was the Rain, Too Much Monkey Business, Yellow Rose of Texas and The Eyes of Texas (medley), She's a Machine, Do the Vega, Tiger Man* (recorded live at NBC for the Elvis special, for which this album was released through Singer Sewing Centers)   RCA PRS 279

December
1968   Elvis (TV Special)
            *Trouble and Guitar Man, Lawdy, Miss Clawdy and Baby, What You Want Me to
            do, Dialogue, Medley: Heartbreak Hotel, Hound Dog, All Shook Up, Can't Help
            Falling in Love, Jailhouse Rock, Dialogue, Love Me Tender, Dialogue, Where
            Could I go But to the Lord, Up Above My Head and Saved, Dialogue, Blue
            Christmas, Dialogue, One Night, Memories, Medley: Nothingville, Dialogue, Big
            Boss Man, Guitar Man, Little Egypt, Trouble, Guitar Man, If I Can Dream*
                                                                        RCA LPM 4088

May
1969   From Elvis in Memphis
            *Wearin' That Loved On Look, Only the Strong Survive, I'll Hold You in My Heart,
            Long Black Limousine, It Keeps Right on A-Hurtin', I'm Movin' On, Power of My
            Love, Gentle on My Mind, After Loving You, True Love Travels on a Gravel Road,
            Any Day Now, In the Ghetto*
                                                                        RCA LSP 4155

November
1969   From Memphis to Vegas/From Vegas to Memphis (2-record set)
            *Blue Suede Shoes, Johnny B. Goode, All Shook Up, Are You Lonesome Tonight,
            Hound Dog, I Can't Stop Loving You, My Babe, Mystery Train and Tiger Man
            (medley), Words, In the Ghetto, Suspicious Minds, Can't Help Falling in Love,
            Inherit the Wind, This is the Story, Stranger in My Own Home Town, A Little Bit
            of Green, And the Grass Won't Pay No Mind, Do You Know Who I Am, From a
            Jack to a King, The Fair's Moving On, You'll Think of Me, Without Love*
                                                                        RCA LSP 6020

May
1970   On Stage: February, 1970
            *See See Rider, Release Me, Sweet Caroline, Run-away, The Wonder of You,
            Polk Salad Annie, Yesterday, Proud Mary, Walk a Mile in My Shoes, Let It Be Me*
                                                                        RCA LSP 4362

August
1970   Worldwide 50 Gold Award Hits, Vol. 1.
            *Heartbreak Hotel, I Was the One, I Want You, I Need You, I Love You, Don't Be
            Cruel, Hound Dog, Love Me Tender, Any Way You Want Me, Too Much, Playing
            for Keeps, All Shook Up, That's When Your Heartaches Begin, Loving You,
            Teddy Bear, Jailhouse Rock, Trust Me Nice, I Beg of You, Don't, Wear My Ring
            Around Your Neck, Hard Headed Woman, I Got Stung, A Fool Such As I, A Big
            Hunk o'Love, Stuck on You, A Mess of Blues, It's Now or Never, I Gotta Know,
            Are You Lonesome Tonight, Surrender, I Feel So Bad, Little Sister, Can't Help
            Falling in Love, Rock-a-Hula Baby, Anything That's Part of You, Good Luck
            Charm, She's Not You, Return to Sender, Where Do You Come From, One*

Broken Heart for Sale, Devil in Disguise, Bossa Nova Baby, Kissin' Cousins,
Viva Las Vegas, Ain't That Loving You, Baby, Wooden Heart, Crying in the
Chapel, If I Can Dream, In the Ghetto, Suspicious Minds, Don't Cry, Daddy,
Kentucky Rain; Plus: Excerpts from Elvis Sails   RCA LPM 6401

November

1970   Back in Memphis
              Inherit the Wind, This Is the Story, Stranger in My Own Home Town, A Little Bit
              of Green, The Grass Won't Pay No Mind, Do You Know Who I Am, From a Jack to
              a King, The Fair's Moving On, You'll Think of Me, Without Love   ⋅ RCA LSP 4429

December

1970   Elvis: That's the Way It Is
              I Just Can't Help Believin', Twenty Days and Twenty Nights, How the Web Was
              Woven, Patch It Up, Mary in the Morning, You Don't Have to Say You Love Me,
              You've Lost That Lovin' Feeling, I've Lost Me, You've Lost That Lovin' Feeling,
              I've Lost You, Just Pretend, Stranger in the Crowd, The Next Step Is Love,
              Bridge Over Troubled Water   RCA LSP 4445

September

1971   Elvis: The Other Sides—Worldwide Gold Award Hits, Vol. 2
              Puppet on a String, Witchcraft, Trouble, Poor Boy, I Want To Be Free, Doncha'
              Think It's Time, Young Dreams, The Next Step Is Love, You Don't Have to Say
              You Love Me, Paralyzed, My Wish Came True, When My Blue Moon Turns to
              Gold Again, Lonesome Cowboy, My Baby Left Me, It Hurts Me, I Need Your Love
              Tonight, Tell Me Why, Please Don't Drag That String Around, Young and
              Beautiful, Hot Dog, New Orleans, We're Gonna Move, Crawfish, King Creole,
              I Believe In the Man in the Sky, Dixieland Rock, The Wonder of You, They Remind
              Me Too Much of You, Mean Woman Blues, Lonely Man, Any Day Now, Don't Ask
              My Why, Marie's the Name—His Latest Flame, I Really Don't Want to Know,
              (You're So Square) Baby I Don't Care, I've Lost You, Let Me, Love Me, Got a Lot
              o' Living to Do, Fame and Fortune, Rip It Up, There Goes My Everything, Lover
              Doll, One Night, Just Tell Her Jim Said Hello, Ask Me, Patch It Up, As Long As I
              Have You, You'll Think of Me, Wild in the Country   RCA LPM 6402

December

1971   The Wonderful World of Christmas
              O Come, All Ye Faithful, The First Noel, Winter Wonderland, Silver Bells, On a
              Snowy Christmas Night, It Won't Seem Like Christmas, I'll Be Home on
              Christmas Day, Holly Leaves and Christmas Trees, Merry Christmas Baby, If I
              Get Home on Christmas Day, The Wonderful World of Christmas   RCA LSP 4579

March
1971   Elvis Country
*Snowbird, Tomorrow Never Comes, Little Cabin on the Hill, Whole Lot-ta Shakin'
Goin' On, Funny How Time Slips Away, I Really Don't Want to Know, There Goes
My Everything, It's Your Baby, You Rock It, The Fool, Faded Love, I Washed My
Hands in Muddy Water, Make the World Go Away, I Was Born About Ten
Thousand Years Ago*   RCA LSP 4460

August
1971   Love Letters from Elvis
*Love Letters, When I'm Over You, If I Were You, Got My Mojo Working, Heart of
Rome, Only Believe, This Is Our Dance, Cindy, Cindy, I'll Never Know, Life,
It Ain't No Big Thing*   RCA LSP 4530

March
1972   Elvis—Now
*Help Me Make It Through the Night, Miracle of the Rosary, Hey Jude, Put Your
Hand in the Hand, Until It's Time for You to Go, We Can Make the Morning,
Early Mornin' Rain, Sylvia, Fools Rush In, I Was Born Ten Thousand Years Ago*
                                                                RCA LSP 4671

June
1972   He Touched Me
*He Touched Me, I've Got Confidence, Amazing Grace, Seeing Is Believing, He Is
My Everything, Bosom of Abraham, An Evening Prayer, Lead Me, Guide Me,
There Is No God But God, A Thing Called Love, I, John, Reach Out to Jesus*
                                                                RCA LSP 4690

August
1972   Elvis As Recorded Live at Madison Square Garden (June 10, 1972)
*Introduction: Also sprach Zarathustra, That's All Right, Proud Mary, Never Been
to Spain, You Don't Have to Say You Love Me, You've Lost that Lovin' Feelin,
Polk Salad Annie, Love Me, All Shook Up, Heartbreak Hotel, Medley: (Let Me Be
Your) Teddy Bear and Don't Be Cruel, Love Me Tender, The Impossible Dream,
Introductions by Elvis, Hound Dog, Suspicious Minds, For the Good Times,
American Trilogy, Funny How Time Slips Away, I Can't Stop Loving You, Can't
Help Falling in Love*   RCA LSP 4776

April
1973   Aloha from Hawaii Via Satellite (January 14, 1973)
*Introduction: Also sprach Zarathustra, See See Rider, Burning Love, Something,
You Gave Me a Mountain, Steamroller Blues, My Way, Love Me, Johnny B.
Goode, It's Over, Blue Suede Shoes, I'm So Lonesome I Could Cry, I Can't Stop
Loving You, Hound Dog, What Now My Love, Fever, Welcome to My World,
Suspicious Minds, Introductions by Elvis, I'll Remember You, Medley: Long Tall*

Sally and Whole Lot-ta Shakin' Goin' On, American Trilogy, A Big Hunk o' Love, Can't Help Falling in Love   RCA VPSX-6089

July
1973   ELVIS
            Fool, Where Do I Go From Here, It's Impossible, It's Still Here, I Will Be True, I'll Take You Home Again Kathleen, (That's What You Get) For Lovin' Me, Padre, Don't Think Twice, It's All Right, Love Me, Love the Life I Lead   RCA APL 1-0283

October
1973   Raised On Rock/For Ol' Times Sake
            Raised on Rock, Are You Sincere, Find Out What's Happening, I Miss You, Girl of Mine, For Ol' Times Sake, If You Don't Come Back, Just a Little Bit, Sweet Angeline, Three Corn Patches   RCA APL 1-0388

January
1974   ELVIS: A Legendary Performer, Vol. 1
            That's All Right, I Love You Because (unreleased take), *Heartbreak Hotel, Don't Be Cruel, Love Me* (unreleased live version), *Trying To Get To You* (unreleased live version), *Love Me Tender, (There'll Be) Peace In the Valley, (Now and Then There's) A Fool Such As I, Tonight's All Right for Love* (unreleased song from G.I. Blues), *Are You Lonesome Tonight?* (unreleased live version), *Can't Help Falling in Love, plus excerpts from Elvis' press conference on September 22, 1958.*   RCA CPL 1-0341

May
1974   Good Times
            Take Good Care of Her, Loving Arms, I Got a Feelin' in My Body, If That Isn't Love, She Wears My Ring, I've Got a Thing About You Baby, My Boy, Spanish Eyes, Talk About the Good Times, Good Time Charlie's Got the Blues
                                                                          RCA CPL 1-0475

September
1974   Elvis As Recorded Live On Stage in Memphis
            See See Rider, I Got a Woman, Love Me, Trying to Get to You, Medley: Long Tall Sally, Whole Lot-Ta Shakin' Goin On, Flip, Flop and Fly, Jailhouse Rock and Hound Dog, Why Me Lord, How Great Thou Art, Medley: Blueberry Hill and I Can't Stop Loving You, Help Me, An American Trilogy, Let Me Be There, My Baby Left Me, Lawdy, Miss Clawdy, Can't Help Falling in Love   RCA CPL 1-0606

October
1974   Having Fun with Elvis on Stage
            A Talking Album only—Elvis talking to and with his concert audiences (Album was privately recorded and marketed briefly before RCA bought up the rights)
                                                                          RCA CPM 1-0818

January
1975   Promised Land
            *Promised Land, There's A Honky Tonk Angel (Who Will Take Me Back In), Help
            Me, Mr. Songman, Love Song of the Year, It's Midnight, Your Love's Been a Long
            Time Coming, If You Talk in Your Sleep, Thinking About You, You Asked Me To*
                                                                            RCA APL 1-0873

CAMDEN

April
1969   Elvis Sings "Flaming Star"
            Commercial release of the Presley album (RCA PRS-279) issued as a special
            premium in November 1968 in conjunction with the Singer TV program.
                                                                            RCA CAS-2304

April
1970   Let's Be Friends
            Stay Away, Joe (from Stay Away Joe*), If I'm a Fool, Let's Be Friends, Let's Forget
            About the Stars, Mama (from* Girls! Girls! Girls!*), I'll Be There, Almost (from*
            The Trouble with Girls*), Change of Habit (from* Change of Habit*), Have a Happy
            (from* Change of Habit*)*   RCA CAS-2408

November
1970   Elvis' Christmas Album
            *Blue Christmas, Silent Night, White Christmas, Santa Claus Is Back in Town,
            I'll Be Home for Christmas, If Every Day Was Like Christmas, Here Comes Santa
            Claus, O Little Town of Bethlehem, Santa Bring My Baby Back, Mama Liked the
            Roses*   RCA CAL-2428

November
1970   Almost in Love
            Almost in Love (from Live a Little, Love a Little*), Long Legged Girl (from* Double
            Trouble*), Edge of Reality (from* Live a Little, Love a Little*), My Little Friend, A
            Little Less Conversation (from* Live a Little, Love a Little*), Rubberneckin' (from*
            Change of Habit*), Clean Up Your Own Back Yard (from* The Trouble with Girls*),
            U. S. Male (from* Stay Away, Joe*), Charro! (from* Charro!*), Stay Away, Joe (from*
            Stay Away, Joe*)*   RCA CAS-2440

March
1971   You'll Never Walk Alone
            You'll Never Walk Alone, Who Am I?, Let Us Pray (from Change of Habit*),
            (There'll Be) Peace in the Valley, We Call On Him, I Believe, It Is No Secret (What
            God Can Do), Sing You Children, Take My Hand, Precious Lord*   RCA CALX-2472

August
1971   C'mon Everybody
         *C'mon Everybody, Angel, Easy Come, Easy Go, A Whistling Tune, Follow That
         Dream, King of the Whole Wide World, I'll Take Love, Today, Tomorrow and
         Forever, I'm Not the Marrying Kind, This Is Living*   RCA CAL-2518

November
1971   I Got Lucky
         I Got Lucky (from Kid Galahad*), What a Wonderful Life (from* Follow That
         Dream*), I Need Somebody to Lean On (from* Viva Las Vegas*), Yoga Is As Yoga
         Does (from* Easy Come, Easy Go*), Riding the Rainbow (from* Kid Galahad*), Fools
         Fall in Love, The Love Machine (from* Easy Come, Easy Go*), Home Is Where the
         Heart Is (from* Kid Galahad*), You Gotta Stop (from* Easy Come, Easy Go*), If You
         Think I Don't Need You (from* Viva Las Vegas*)*   RCA CAL-2533

March
1972   Elvis Sings Hits from His Movies, Vol. 1
         Down By the Riverside and When the Saints Go Marching In (from Frankie and
         Johnny*), They Remind Me Too Much of You (from* It Happened at the World's
         Fair*), Confidence, from* Clambake*), Frankie and Johnny (from* Frankie and
         Johnny*), Guitar Man, Long Legged Girl (With the Short Dress On), from* Double
         Trouble*), You Don't Know Me (from* Clambake*), How Would You Like to Be (from*
         It Happened at the World's Fair*), Big Boss Man, Old MacDonald (from* Double
         Trouble*)*   RCA CAS-2567

July
1972   "Burning Love" and Hits from His Movies, Vol. 2
         *Burning Love, Tender Feeling, Am I Ready, Tonight Is So Right for Love,
         Guadalajara, It's A Matter of Time, No More, Santa Lucia, We'll Be Together,
         I Love Only One Girl*   RCA CAS-2595

November
1972   Separate Ways
         *Separate Ways, Sentimental Me, In My Way, I Met Her Today, What Now, What
         Next, Where To, Always on My Mind, I Slipped, I Stumbled, I Feel, Is It So
         Strange, Forget Me Never, Old Shep*   RCA CAS-2611

April
1975   Elvis: Pure Gold
         *Love Me Tender, Loving You, Kentucky Rain, Fever, It's Impossible, Jailhouse
         Rock, Don't Be Cruel, I Got a Woman, All Shook Up, In the Ghetto*   ANL 1-0971
